Outlines

of

Truth

Dear Reader,

This book and other titles are being published with our desire and prayer to be of help in studying the Word of God (2 Tim.2:15).

We would love to hear your remarks; they are appreciated and welcomed! Please contact us at:

Believers Bookshelf, Inc.
P. O. Box 261, Sunbury, Pennsylvania, 17801
USA
www.bbusa.org

Outlines

of

Truth

BY
F. B. HOLE
(Edited)

Believers Bookshelf, Inc.
P. O. Box 261, Sunbury, Pennsylvania, 17801
USA
<u>www.bbusa.org</u>

OUTLINES OF TRUTH

F. B. HOLE (Edited)

2007

Published and Distributed

By

Believers Bookshelf, Inc.

P. O. Box 261, Sunbury, Pennsylvania, 17801

USA

www.bbusa.org

Publishers and distributors of select Christian literature.
A nonprofit corporation since 1966.

Copyright © 2007 by
Believers Bookshelf, Inc. [USA] *All rights reserved.*
ISBN-10   0-88172-336-3
ISBN-13   978-0-88172-336-6

Available through

Literature ministries as listed on www.bbusa.org

USA: Believers Bookshelf, Inc., P. O. Box 261, Sunbury, PA 17801
Canada: Believer's Bookshelf, 5205 Regional Rd. #81, Unit 3, Beamsville, Ontario L0R 1B3
UK: Chapter Two Fountain House, Conduit Mews. London, SE18 7AP
St. Kitts: Believer's Bookshelf, P. O. Box 777, Shadwell Heights, Basseterre
Jamaica: Ocean View Bible Camp, Southfield P. O., St. Elizabeth
Egypt: Brethren Bookstore, 3 Anga Hanem St., Shoubra, Cairo 11231
Ghana: Christian Literature Service, P. O. Box GP 20872, Accra
Nigeria: Christian Literature Depot, P. O. Box 436, Ijeshatedo, Surulere, Lagos

For updated listing, please visit www.bbusa.org

We appreciate the prayerful support of our brethren and the work of the
Production Team: Roger P. Daniel, Larry Rosen and André N. Hanna.

Cover Design © by Larry Rosen and André N. Hanna
Cover Photo by Mary Daniel
Printed in the USA

TABLE OF CONTENTS

THANKING THE LORD
"Thus far the LORD has helped us" (1 Sam.7:12).

We thank the Lord for His help in publishing this new edition of *Outlines of Truth** with its new cover, new page layout and overall presentation.

We thank the Lord for exercising individuals and assemblies to pray for this ministry, its Council and staff.

Furthermore, we thank the Lord for each individual He provided who had a role in the publication and distribution of this book, especially those who showed devotedness and diligence throughout the entire production process.

This book is prayerfully committed to the Lord for His blessing.

For the Council and staff of   *André N. Hanna,* MD
Believers Bookshelf, Inc. USA

∾

*This title was published previously by *Believers Bookshelf* in a saddle-stitched booklet format, ISBN# 0-88172-143-3.

THE CHRISTIAN UPDATE SERIES

The *Christian Update Series* consists of outstanding religious writings of 19th and early 20th century authors, which writings have been edited to make them easier to read and understand.

We have a gold mine of truth from these God-gifted writers who opened up for us the Scriptures in a way not known for 1500 years. Unfortunately, today, many of these writings are not being read or when read, are not easily understood by many. One reason is the style of writing has dramatically changed in the last century from a strong emphasis on literary beauty (with long and involved sentence structure) to emphasis on simplicity and readability. Also, many words have changed meaning or are no longer in common use.

Therefore, believing it to be the Lord's leading, I am editing some of these writings to make them easier to understand, while maintaining to the best of my ability the writer's exactness of meaning and as much of his style as possible. References to papers no longer in print and to events no longer well known, have been omitted. Also, some footnotes have been added as needed for clarification. However, since the original authors are no longer living and editing errors are occasionally possible either through misunderstanding or in leaving something out, questions as to fine points of the authors' doctrinal beliefs should always be referred to the original text.

I pray this *Christian Update Series* will help those who read it to grow in the truth and give them a greater appreciation of their Lord and Savior, Jesus Christ. Also, I pray that any who read this series who do not know Jesus Christ as Savior will be convicted of their sinful condition and put their trust in Jesus as their Lord and Savior.

Roger P. Daniel

PREFACE

Mr. Frank B. Hole's *Outlines Of Truth* has been chosen as Volume Six of the *Christian Update Series* because of its unique presentation of basic Bible truth. Every Christian needs to know the truths presented in this book before he or she can understand even the basics of what God would have us know. In fact, most differences of opinion among Christians about the Bible result from not understanding and differentiating between the things presented herein.

Mr. Hole was born in England in 1874. For many years before his death in 1964, he was a well known, beloved and respected Bible teacher among the English assemblies.

Mr. Hole wrote a number of pamphlets and also three well-known books—*The Great Salvation, Foundations of Faith* and *Outlines of Truth,* which is herein edited into "Americanized" English. Another pamphlet by Mr. Hole entitled *Assembly Principles* is Volume 4 of the Christian Update Series, while *The Great Salvation* is Volume 5.

I pray the Lord will further use this extremely helpful book, now in its edited form, to help many of the Lord's dear people to more clearly understand what God has for them in the Bible.

Most Scripture quotes are from the *New King James Version* (NKJV), used by permission. The very accurate J.N. Darby translation is used in places to help insure fidelity to the original Greek or Hebrew.

Every effort is made to include many references throughout this book. Therefore, please read this book with an open Bible. You don't want to get Mr. Hole's or my opinion *about* the Bible, *but the clear truth of Scripture.* This can only be obtained by making sure everything you read is solidly backed up by the Word of God as revealed to us by the Holy Spirit through prayer and study.

Roger P. Daniel

INTRODUCTION

The following chapters are brief outlines of Bible truths connected with the foundations of Christianity. We can't really appreciate our standing or position before God unless we have some understanding of these very important subjects. May the Lord bless this study to each of us and cause us to have a greater appreciation of our Lord and Savior, Jesus Christ.

∾

NOTES

Chapter 1

FAITH AND WORKS

Many people believe that faith and works are not compatible with each other in Christianity, but this is not true. It *is* true that we are not *saved* by human merit or good works, but by faith in the Lord Jesus Christ. Yet, the Bible speaks of a kind of good works that is in complete harmony with faith and, in fact, is closely connected with it. It also speaks of bad works.

In Colossians 1:21 we find "wicked works"—the terrible outcome of the fallen, corrupt and sinful nature of the children of Adam. These works are the bad fruit of a bad tree.

In Hebrews 9:14 we see "dead works" which are works such as religious duties and observances done in the hope of obtaining blessing and eternal life. They are man's "righteousnesses" which are as "filthy rags" in God's sight (Isa.64:6). These works are the product of a bad tree when it has been cultivated to the utmost, but the fruit is still bad because no amount of skill can produce oranges from a thorn bush.

In Titus 2:7-9, we find "good works," and these works are strongly enforced upon Christians. These works are the fruit of that new eternal life and divine nature of which the Christian partakes (2 Pet. 1:4), which has its vitality in faith and the Holy Spirit as its power. These works are the good fruit which grows on the good tree.

In Romans 3-5 we see that justification before God is
only on the principle of faith. "A man is justified by faith
apart from the deeds of the law" [of Moses] (Rom.3:28).
On the other hand, James 2 clearly tells us that justification *as a public thing in this world before men* is mainly
by works. "You see then that a man is justified by works
and not by faith only" (Jas.2:24).

If you carefully study these chapters in Romans and
James, you will see the harmony that exists between faith
and works. Both passages use Abraham as the great Old
Testament example that supports the truth expressed. God
called Abraham to become "the father of all those who
believe" (Rom.4:11) and faith was a living reality in his
life with God. He *believed* God that he and Sarah would
have a son when it was humanly impossible, and God
counted that belief as righteousness (Gen.15:4-6).

Years later, we see a great *work* of faith when in simple
obedience to God, Abraham went to Mount Moriah to
sacrifice Isaac *who was that promised son* from whom
would come a great nation (Gen.22:1-19). He believed
God could and would raise the dead. This public act
proved his faith in God *before men*. It was the *outward*
evidence of his *inward* faith.

Like the story of one man inside a hollow ball who
insisted the ball was concave and another man outside
who insisted it was convex, Paul in Romans gives us the
inside view and says "by faith," while James, viewing
things externally, says "by works," but Paul and James
don't disagree with each other in so saying.

You may be wondering just what faith is. A good definition is "believing what God says *because God says it.*" Faith is like a window. It lets in the sunshine. The sunshine is shining on the outside wall, but it can only light up a dark room when there is a window. Divine light comes streaming into our souls when we "believe God" like Abraham did. However, true faith goes even beyond this. It means not only to *have* the light, *but to completely rest on the One (Jesus) whom the light reveals to us.*

A missionary was having difficulty finding a word for *trusting* or *believing* in the local language. One day he called a local Christian and when seated on a chair, asked him what he was doing. The native replied in the local language that he was "resting." It wasn't the word the missionary wanted, so he lifted both feet off the floor and again asked the native what he was doing now. The Christian replied, "You are now *completely resting*; you are *trusting*," using a word new to the missionary. That was the word he wanted. Thus, faith is resting completely on Christ *with both feet off the ground.*

Let's look further at Romans 4:5 where we are told a believer's faith is counted for righteousness. What does that mean?

First, we shouldn't think of it in a *commercial* sense as though we bring God so much faith and in exchange, we receive so much righteousness. Secondly, neither should we think of it in a *chemical* sense that our faith is transformed into righteousness. Rather, Abraham is the great example of what is meant. He and we are considered by God as righteous in view of faith. Faith brings in all the justifying-merits of the blood of Christ. As a result, we are eternally reckoned as if we had never sinned: we are declared righteous, the meaning of *justification*. In fact, believing on the Lord Jesus Christ (faith) is the first right (or righteous) thing that a person can do.

Philippians 2:12 tells us to "work out your own salvation" and thus might seem to be in conflict with what we have just said, and with Ephesians 2:8-9 which says that we are saved by grace "through faith ... not of works lest anyone should boast." However, the subject of Philippians 1 and 2 is the practical walk of the believer, and all verses should be interpreted in relation to their context. Many difficulties faced these Philippian believers, but the Lord Jesus was their great Example. Conscious of their weakness, they were to work out their own salvation *from the various forms of evil that threatened them.* God would help: by the Holy Spirit, He works *in us* and *we work outward.*

We must be careful to not indiscriminately preach "only believe." Paul consistently preached "repentance towards God and faith toward our Lord Jesus Christ" (Acts 20:21). When speaking to the anxious jailer of Philippi in whose soul a work of repentance was already proceeding, Paul only said, "Believe on the Lord Jesus Christ" (Acts 16:31). There, "only believe" was quite in place. In less than an hour after his salvation, the jailor performed his first good work (v.33) *which was the fruit and proof of his faith.*

In Acts 26:20, Paul further told us that he preached that people should "repent, turn to God, and do works befitting repentance." This is very important. If a person professes to be saved, we can correctly demand that the change be evident in his daily life before we fully accept his profession. But, again, the good works are a *result* of the change that grace has worked within the heart.

James 2:17-20 speaks of "dead faith" which is merely human faith or *head-belief,* but not the living faith that finds its source in God. The *demons* have this kind of faith (v.19). It may *outwardly* appear to be real faith, but it does not have good works. It is only an imitation—a dead and useless tree. *There is no fruit.*

An example is given in John 2:23-25 and 6:66-71. People believed in the miracles performed by Jesus—a head faith—but not in *Him* and thus turned away from Him. Peter, on the other hand, had living faith. Judas Iscariot is the example of a man with the highest form of profession, but with no faith at all.

When professing Christians do little or no good works, only God can really know what is the true state of the soul (2 Tim.2:19). Good works are like the hands on the face of a clock. They indicate the result of the activity inside.

Faith is the power of the activity. Maybe such people are only professors like a child's toy watch with the hands painted on the face and no insides at all. Or maybe something has gone wrong with the works within: the true Christian has sunk into a low and worldly condition and thus is "shortsighted even to blindness, and has forgotten that he was cleansed from his old sins" (2 Pet.1:9). Still, "a tree is known by its fruit" (Mt.12:33).

Since the Christian is the world's Bible, we can well understand the stress laid on good works in Scripture (Eph.2:10; 1 Pet.2:9-12; Titus 2).

We must clearly understand, however, that the believer's works on earth will not affect his place in heaven since our place in heaven is only on the basis of the work of Christ. The Father "has qualified us to be partakers of the inheritance of the saints in the light" (Col.1:12). All is by grace. Every true Christian has the title to an equally good place in heaven.

On the other hand, our *works* will greatly affect our place in the 1000-year-long kingdom of our Lord Jesus Christ (the Millennium) as shown in the parables of the *talents* (Mt.25:14-30) and the *pounds* or *minas* (Lk.19:11-27). 2 Peter 1:5-11 further tells us to abound in every spiritual grace and work, "for so an entrance will be supplied to you *abundantly* into the everlasting kingdom of our Lord and Savior Jesus Christ." There *are degrees of position in the Millennium.*

∾

Chapter 2

PEACE AND DELIVERANCE

Romans 5:1 tells us that "having been justified by faith, we have peace with God through our Lord Jesus Christ," whereas Paul says in Romans 7:24-25, "O wretched man that I am! Who will deliver me from this body of death? I thank God—through Jesus Christ our Lord."

Both peace with God and deliverance from sin and the flesh (old nature) within, are great blessings which the gospel brings to all of us, but they are distinct. It is important to understand the difference between them and also how each is made our own. The cross of Christ is, of course, the great basis of both.

The results of sin are seen both externally and internally. Externally, sin has broken the once-happy link that united man to his Creator. Satan used sin to cut the line of communication between man and God in the Garden of Eden. Sin has thus brought in distance, estrangement and enmity *on man's side* against God.

Internally, the wreck is just as complete. Chaos reigns in the mind and heart of every sinner. Instead of being joyous, free and moving in intelligent subjection in the sunlight of God's favor, he is in bondage. Sin is his master. His own spirit is no longer in control of his mind and body, but he is at the mercy of many evil passions and lusts.

Romans 1-3 shows us the terrible condition into which sin has plunged man as to his relations with God. Then God sets forth the divine remedy which is the death and resurrection of Christ and, *for faith,* the result of this remedy *is peace with God.*

Now read Romans 7. See the *internal* confusion and anarchy, the tangle of conflicting desires, emotions and struggles as a result of sin. But we can emerge out of this mess thanks to the cross of Christ and the Holy Spirit's power (Rom.8:1-4). We thus can be "delivered from this body of death."

Peace, then, is with God and is the result of having all our relations with Him placed on a righteous and completely satisfactory foundation through the work of Christ on the cross.

Deliverance, on the other hand, is "from this body of death," our corrupt old nature which all of us carry about within ourselves as a result of sin in the flesh.

Both peace and deliverance are declared to be "through Jesus Christ our Lord." His cross is the complete answer to all our guilt. Thus, we who believe are justified by God (Rom.3:25-26). His cross also is the full condemnation of all we were in ourselves as self-destroyed children of Adam (Rom.6:6; 8:3), so deliverance might reach us in the power of the risen Christ.

Although peace is always preceded by anxiety due to seeing one's dangerous position before God, it is obtained only *by faith* (Rom.5:1). Our eyes were suddenly opened to gaze in faith on the once crucified and now risen Savior.

We saw every question settled, every obstacle removed and every cloud between us and God rolled away. The result was peace!

Deliverance, although by faith, is largely linked with *experience.* We wade through the mud of Romans 7 to reach the solid ground found at the end of the chapter. We learn the useful but painful lessons of *no good in the flesh* (the old nature) (v.18) and no power in our best desires (v.23) even when those desires come from the new nature within, called here "the law of my mind" and "the inward man." Only when these lessons are learned does the person who is weary of sin and self, look for an outside Deliverer and finds one in the Lord Jesus Christ.

Such deliverance is found in both the knowledge of the meaning of Christ's cross as the complete condemnation of sin in the flesh and in the power of the Holy Spirit who makes Christ a living, bright reality to us, so that, under this warm influence, order begins to appear out of chaos and victory is obtained over sin.

It is possible to have one's sins forgiven and yet not have peace. *Forgiveness* depends only on simple *faith in Christ.* "Whoever believes in Him will receive remission of sins" (Acts 10:43), whereas *peace* depends on faith in the gospel of God, which sets before us a Savior "who has been delivered for our offenses and has been raised for our justification" (Rom.4:25, JND). Thus, one may simply believe in Christ and completely trust in Him as a poor sinner without believing with equal simplicity the gospel message which sets before us, not only Himself, but His work and its results.

Too many people pay too much attention to their feelings and not enough to the unchanging gospel and thus don't have peace, although they fully trust in Christ. However, such a state of things is not what God intends or what Scripture plans for us. Rather, it is the result of poor teaching or of unbelief on our part.

Romans 1-5 deals with *peace* while Romans 6-8 deals with *deliverance,* so Scripture does not indicate that peace and deliverance must be received together. It would seem with most Christians that the question of *sins* and how to meet God, entirely fills the vision until peace is known, and *then* the Holy Spirit raises the question of *sin* and the *flesh,* and victory over both. However, some believers testify that they received peace and deliverance essentially at one time. Scripture does not lay down any set rule.

Can a person be in the miserable condition of Romans 7 and yet have peace with God? Look at what that chapter does *not* mention. From verses 7-24 there is no mention of the redeeming work of Christ or of the Holy Spirit. Thus, these painful exercises are evidently those of one born again and with a new nature, but in his conscience, still under the Law of Moses.* In this worst-case example (for Scripture often uses worst-case examples) absolutely nothing is right: He evidently doesn't have peace with God. Yet, believers who have true peace with God may be living in the gloom of failure and worldliness and thus be miserable.

---

* *Editor's Note:* Mr. Hole here makes reference to new birth and the Holy Spirit, which, without considerable explanation, could cause confusion and possibly detract from the discussion. Hence, these two lines are left out of this edited edition. These matters are much more thoroughly discussed in Mr. Hole's *The Great Salvation*, Volume 5 of *The Christian Update Series.*

If a believer never has such an experience, something is wrong with him. To "get into Romans 7" is a sign of spiritual progress because it indicates a sensitive conscience and a real desire to walk a holy pathway. The painful lessons learned are beneficial. Just as one needs soul-anxiety to get peace, one needs a Romans 7 experience to get that deliverance from sin which leads to a healthy, vigorous Christian life. [Note that some of us, saved as a child, brought up in the Lord's things, may not have the consciousness of sins that others converted later in life may have. Thus the Romans 7 experience may be less, Ed.]

We get such deliverance by simply looking away from self to Christ. Note all the "I's" and "me's" in Romans 7:7-24 and then the sudden change in verse 24. Sickened and hopeless, Paul stops looking at himself and seeks an outside Deliverer: "*Who* will deliver me?"

We don't get this deliverance once and for all at a definite moment. *Peace*, the result of receiving God's testimony as to the finished work of Christ, often comes like a flash of lightning, but *deliverance* depends on both Christ's work *for* us and on the Holy Spirit's work *in* us. The Spirit's work is gradual, and He can be quenched and grieved. There is a moment when we cry out, "O wretched man that I am: who will deliver me," and we begin to realize what it means to be "in Christ Jesus" (Rom.8:1). Then we first taste the sweet liberty resulting from coming under the control of "the Spirit of life in Christ Jesus" (Rom.8:2). That is the moment deliverance begins, *but it has to be maintained and actually increased.*

Therefore, don't struggle against the power of indwelling sin. Look away to the great Deliverer. Lose yourself in the warm beams of His love and glory: *that is real deliverance.* The following allegory illustrates this. The drops of water in the ocean looked up at the clouds and longed to leave the cold, restless depths and soar in the heavens with them. So they determined to try. They called on the wind to help them.

The wind caused great waves to smash against the rocks until the drops, now broken into a fine spray, felt that they would be driven upward to the clouds. But no, back they fell on the cold, dark waves. At last they sighed, "It will never be" and the wind stopped. Then the sun shone brightly on the calm sea and almost before they knew it, the drops were lifted by its mighty power and without effort on their part, found themselves floating in the heavenlies in the warmth of the sun.

Thus is deliverance. Keep in the warm sunshine of the love of Christ and you will soon be saying, "I thank God—through Jesus Christ our Lord" (Rom.7:25).

Chapter 3
SAFETY AND SANCTIFICATION

When God called Israel out of Egypt, He first ensured their safety from judgment by sheltering them beneath the blood of the slain lamb (Ex.12). Then He sanctified the firstborn who had been sheltered (Ex.13:1-2). Safety and sanctification are likewise connected in the New Testament. For instance, in John 17, the Lord first declared the past and future safety of His own, "Holy Father, keep through Your name those whom You have given Me .... Those whom You gave Me, I have kept" (vv.11-12). Immediately afterwards, He prayed concerning their sanctification (vv.17-19).

We thus see that God wants the believer to be both safe and sanctified. Don't, however, connect your safety with your growth in grace, or so widely separate the two as to make them a first and second blessing with possibly years of experience between.

Although there is no difficulty in understanding the term safety, *sanctification* is one of the most widely misunderstood words in Scripture. Some think it means *sanctimonious* or to *become very holy*. It does not! Its primary meaning throughout Scripture is *to set apart* for the service and pleasure of God. Exodus 40:10 speaks of *sanctifying* the altar. [Note: NKJV and JND use *hallow* or *consecrate*, essentially similar terms, Ed.] In John 17:19, the Lord said "I sanctify Myself" and in 1 Peter 3:15, we are told to "sanctify the Lord God in your hearts."

How can a wood or metal object be sanctified [or, consecrated]? They can't be made holy because they have no mind or character, but they can be *set apart* for divine use. In the same sense, the already completely holy Lord Jesus has set Himself apart in heaven for our sakes and we can set God apart in our hearts by always giving Him that place of supremacy and honor which is rightly His.

Likewise, when sanctification is connected with us believers, it has the same meaning of being set apart for the pleasure and service of God; God claiming for Himself those whom He has sheltered by blood (Ex.13:2).

Note carefully that our sanctification has two aspects. The first is *positional and absolute*—an act of God with which we start our Christian career. The second is *practical and progressive* and it continues and deepens throughout our pathway on earth.

Those scriptures which speak of the believer as *already* sanctified fall under our first heading. For instance, in 1 Corinthians 1:2, Paul wrote to "those who are sanctified in Christ Jesus." Then in 1 Corinthians 6:11, Paul says, "But you were washed, but you were sanctified, but you were justified in the name of the Lord Jesus and by the Spirit of our God."

The Corinthian Christians had not advanced far in their practical sanctification: they were blameworthy in many respects, but Paul doesn't hesitate to remind them that they *had been sanctified* just as they had been washed and justified. They had been set apart for God.

In Hebrews 10:14, JND, we read that "by one offering, He has perfected in perpetuity *the sanctified*." Are these a group of especially holy believers? No! They are all Christians, without distinction—those set apart for God by the one sacrifice of our Lord Jesus Christ.

Now look at 1 Thessalonians 4:3; Ephesians 5:25-26 and 2 Timothy 2:21. "This is the will of God, your sanctification ... Christ also loved the Church and gave Himself for her, that He might sanctify and cleanse her ... If anyone cleanses himself from the latter, he will be a vessel for honor, sanctified and useful for the Master."

In these Scriptures *sanctification* still has its root-meaning of *setting apart*, but it is now an object of attainment or desire, something which is God's *intention* for His people, something that Christ *is doing* for His Church today, something which we are to individually seek and which will be ours if we respond to the divine instructions. This is practical and progressive sanctification.

On what do these things depend? *Safety* is always related to the infinite worth and value of the atoning work of Christ and to His power to keep. Our attainments in practical holiness after salvation, important as they are in their place, *have nothing to do with our safety.* On that fateful night in Egypt (Ex.12), no firstborn son would have been spared if his father had tacked a paper to the door post giving his son's excellence of character and progress in behavior. The safety of every firstborn depended *solely* on the sprinkled blood. Likewise, our safety, forgiveness and justification depend entirely on the precious blood of Christ. We are forgiven "through His name" (Acts 10:43); we are justified "by His blood" (Rom.5:9).

The positional aspect of sanctification is also founded on the work of Christ. By His one offering, we are sanctified. It is also connected with the Holy Spirit. We are "elect ... in sanctification of the Spirit" (1 Pet.1:2). *By the Spirit,* we are born again and in believing the truth, we are sealed by that same Spirit. In virtue of all this, we are set apart for God.

The practical and progressive aspect of sanctification depends on the truth, on God's Word. John 17:17 says to "sanctify them by Your truth; Your Word is truth." In Ephesians 5:26, it is "by the Word." Thus, diligence and purpose of heart in departing from sin are necessary for this aspect of sanctification.

If we "walk in the Spirit" (Gal.5:16), we won't fulfill the wishes of the flesh. Christ is our Object and we are brought under the influence of the truth of God's Word and thereby practically set apart for God in both mind and affections. This setting apart goes on day by day.

Some, in their desire to keep us humble and walking aright, tell us that our degree of attainment in practical sanctification determines the degree of our safety. They feel that if we disconnect safety and sanctification, people will *think* they're saved, but live as they like. *But we do not disconnect the two.* God separates to Himself all those whom He shelters from judgment. No sheltered one is left in the world under the power of sin. However, we do *distinguish* the two because Scripture distinguishes them.

Is our sanctification so frail that we must be kept in perilous uncertainty so we won't shatter it? Is it necessary to terrify little children to make them behave? Is this method the only way to reach the desired end? Is it even the *best* way? No! Then why should we think that God has to terrorize His children? The truth is that all proper conduct flows from the knowledge that we *are safe* and from the correct understanding of *what* we are separated to.

Another false belief is that good progress in practical sanctification improves the believer's title to a place in heaven. Near the close of a life of holy living and devoted service, Paul said that "to depart and be with Christ ... is far better" (Phil.1:23). To a dying robber, just converted, and with only a few hours of holy living to his credit, Jesus said, "Today you will be with Me in paradise" (Lk.23:43). *Both were equally sure of heaven,* based only on the finished work of Christ and the sure Word of God.

The believer *starts* with complete fitness for heaven. We thank the Father "who has qualified us to be partakers of the inheritance of the saints in the light" (Col.1:12). He is not *making* us fit: He *has already made us fit for heaven.*

However, good progress in practical sanctification *improves our fitness for earth.* Thereby, we are better able to take our proper place as witnesses and servants of Christ in this world.

Progressive sanctification is not received at any one particular time or by some special act of faith. Of course, we must *have* faith in the fact that we are already set apart by God for Himself, but we don't *attain* this faith by some mighty act or effort. Faith does act, but faith itself is an abiding and continuous thing. I *have* believed, but I also believe today.

The truth sanctifies and God's Word is truth (Jn.17:17). The Holy Spirit also sanctifies. He is the sanctifying Power because it is He who guides us into all truth (Jn. 16:13). The truth presents Christ to us and shows us His glory. Then, by faith, as we behold Him, we are changed into His image—from one degree of glory to another (2 Cor.3:17-18). *That is progressive sanctification!*

Every true Christian can speak of himself as being sanctified. "Of Him are you in Christ Jesus, who became for us wisdom from God—and righteousness *and sanctification* and redemption" (1 Cor.1:30). You can speak of yourself as being sanctified with the same confidence that you can speak of yourself being redeemed.

On the other hand, no believer can ever correctly claim to be *practically* sanctified. Those who are most Christlike—farthest along in practical sanctification—are the last ones to say so, because *Christ*, not attainment, fills their vision. As with Paul (Phil.3:8), the excellency of the knowledge of Christ Jesus, their Lord, is their pursuit, and if they speak of themselves at all, it is to say, "Not that I have already attained, or am already perfected" (Phil. 3:12).

1 Thessalonians 5:22-23 is sometimes thought to speak of perfect believers who are beyond the reach of temptation. It says. "Abstain from every form of evil. Now may the God of peace Himself sanctify you completely; and may your whole spirit, soul and body be preserved blameless at the coming of our Lord Jesus Christ." However, the context of this verse shows that to be sanctified completely does not mean that the old nature is completely gone. Paul desired that all of his converts have all three of

their parts—the whole man—so practically set apart to God that they would be kept from *every form* of evil.

Nothing less than this should be the object of our prayerful desire even now. "If we say that we have no sin, we deceive ourselves and the truth is not in us" (1 Jn.1:8). Thus, if the old nature isn't eliminated, no believer can consider himself perfect or beyond the reach of sin [and if he still sins, he *must* still have the old nature because only the old nature in a believer can sin, Ed.]

Some wonder why Scripture puts so much emphasis on positional or absolute sanctification, which all the believers automatically have. The reason is because of its great importance to us. The *law* set before us an ideal to strive to gain, but in contrast, God's way *in grace* is to show us what we *are* by His own sovereign choice so we will seek to be consistent with what we are.

Two boys are born on the same day. One is a king's son and is set apart from birth to a high place and a high office. The other is born poor. Why is the young prince constantly reminded that he is the son of a king? Is there any practical benefit in it? Indeed! The two boys may often walk the same streets, but their practical life and behavior are very different. The prince is practically separated from many low and vulgar ways because, *by birth,* he was set apart to a kingly place. In the same way, we can never be too often reminded that by the redeeming work of Christ and by the Holy Spirit's work and indwelling, *we have been set apart for God. Nothing else will be more likely to produce holy living!*

NOTES

Chapter 4

LAW AND GRACE

"The law was given through Moses, but grace and truth came through Jesus Christ ... Sin shall not have dominion over you, for you are not under the law but under grace" (Jn.1:17; Rom.6:14).

In one respect, law and grace are alike because both set before us a very high standard. In all other respects, they are complete opposites. At Mount Sinai (Ex.19–20), God plainly and clearly gave His righteous and holy demands. If men obeyed, they were blessed, but if they disobeyed, they came under the law's solemn curse (Gal.3:10). Israel broke the law and deserved its curse even before the tables of stone had time to reach them (Ex.32). If God hadn't then dealt with Israel in mercy, they would have instantly perished.

Grace, on the other hand, means that blessing is available to all because all God's righteous and holy demands have been met in Christ's death and resurrection. Forgiveness of sins and the gift of the Holy Spirit are granted to all who believe.

The very essence (nature) of the law is *demand,* whereas the essence of grace is *supply.* Under law, God, so to speak, stands before us and says, *"Give!* Render to Me your love and dutiful obedience." Under grace, He stands and says, *"Take!* Receive of My love and saving power." Law says, "Do and live," whereas grace says, "Live and do."

We believers today are not under law but under grace. This came to pass "when the fullness of the time had come, God sent forth His Son, born of a woman, born under the law, to *redeem* those who were under the law, that we might receive the adoption as sons" (Gal.4:4-5). That word *redemption* has made the change! But that involved the death of the Redeemer. He had to be made a curse for us by dying on a tree (Gal.3:13). As a result, the believer can consider himself "dead to the law" (Rom.7:4) because he died in the death of his Representative, the Lord Jesus.

The law didn't die; rather, never was its majesty so upheld as when Jesus died beneath its curse! However, two things did happen. First, because the law was magnified and its curse borne, God suspended His wrath and proclaimed grace to all mankind. Secondly, having died to the law in the person of his great Representative, the believer is "married to Another—to Him who was raised from the dead" (Rom.7:4). The believer is now controlled by another Power, the risen Son of God.

Thus, the law is not the *ground* of a sinner's justification. He is justified by grace, by faith in the blood of Christ (Rom.3–4). Neither is the law the believer's rule of life. Christ is that! Our links are with Him, not with the law (Rom.7:4). Carefully read Galatians 3–4.

The Galatian Christians were converted under the gospel of the grace of God, but were turned aside by Judaizing troublemakers who were "zealous of the law" and taught circumcision and law keeping. Paul told them the law was a temporary arrangement (Gal.3:17) to show up Israel's sins (Gal.3:19) and to act as a schoolmaster or

tutor "up to Christ" (Gal. 3:24, JND). When Christ came
and accomplished redemption and gave the Holy Spirit,
the believer leaves the position of an under-age child or a
servant and becomes a son in the divine household and is
thus placed in the liberty of grace (Gal.4:1-7).

Since the grace-platform to which we have been lifted is
so much higher than the law-platform which we have left,
to go back even in mind to the law, is to *fall*. "You have
fallen from grace" (Gal.5:4) is Paul's words to such as do
this.

The parable of the prodigal son in Luke 15:11-32 illustrates this point. The returning son said to his father,
"Make me like one of your hired servants" (v.19). His
thoughts didn't rise above law. However, he was received
in pure grace and was given the son's place inside the
house. Suppose a few days later, he began to work as a
servant and conform to the servant's laws because he
wanted to retain his father's affection and the place of
privilege so freely given him. He would thus *fall from
grace* and actually grieve his father since the son's actions
would really be a vote of *no confidence* in him. We thus
need to have our hearts *"established* by grace" (Heb.13:9).

Some feel grace came in to help us keep the law so we
might go to heaven that way, but this is a completely
wrong concept. Keeping the law never entitled a person to
heaven, but only not to die. When a lawyer asked the Lord
what he had to do to inherit eternal life, he was referred to
the law. Upon giving a correct summary of its demands,
Jesus answered, "You have answered rightly; this do and
you will live" (Lk.10:25-28). Heaven isn't mentioned
because the only reward for law-keeping is life on earth.

Secondly, grace didn't come in to help us keep the law, but to bring us salvation from its curse by Another bearing that curse for us, as seen in Galatians 3. Also read Romans 3 and notice that when the law has convicted and closed man's mouth (vv.9-19), then grace through righteousness justifies *without the law* (vv.20-24).

In 1 Timothy 1 *law* is used to convict the ungodly (vv. 9-10) and then the gospel of grace presents Christ Jesus who "came into the world to save sinners" (v.15)—not to help sinners keep the law so they could attempt to save themselves!

Why was the law given? Romans 3:19 tells us that the law was given so "every mouth may be stopped and all the world may become guilty before God." Further, "the law entered that the offense might abound ... it was added because of transgressions" (Rom.5:20; Gal.3:19). It has and is achieving its purpose. It can convict and silence the most obstinately self-conceited religionist so grace alone can save him.

Grace, personified in Jesus, has borne the curse of the broken law, thereby redeeming from its curse all who believe in Jesus (Gal.3:13). Further, grace has redeemed us from being under the law itself and has placed all our relationships with God on a new footing (Gal.4:4-6). *However, the law itself is neither annulled nor set aside.* Its majesty was never more clearly upheld than when Jesus suffered as a Substitute under its curse! Multitudes will shrink with fear before its accusations at the day of judgment (Rom.2:12).

The law is not the believer's rule of life. If a believer tries to use the law in this way, he falls from grace, because grace *teaches* as well as saves (Tit.2:11-14). Such a believer also lowers the divine standard because *Christ*, not law, is the believer's standard. Further, he gets hold of the wrong motive power.

Fear may make a person try to keep the law and to regulate the power of the old nature, but the Holy Spirit is the only motive-Power that really can control the flesh and conform the person to Christ (Gal.5:16-18). Lastly, he damages the relationships in which he stands by grace. Though a son in the liberty of the Father's heart and house, he insists on putting himself under the servant's rules!

Some people fear the teaching that a Christian isn't under law will lead to all kinds of wickedness. It *would* if a person became a Christian without new birth, repentance, the gift of the Holy Spirit and coming under the influence of grace. However, no one is a Christian without these things. Therefore, it isn't necessary to *make* Christians live holy lives by keeping them under the threat of the law as if they only had a pig's nature and had to be kept by force out of the mud.

The truth is, although still having the old nature, the believer also has the new nature that cannot sin. He has the Holy Spirit to lead him. Hence, the believer may be safely put under grace because it is grace that subdues. Scripture says, "Sin shall not have dominion over you, for you are not under the law but under grace" (Rom.6:14).

Unsaved people may attempt to use grace as an excuse for wickedness, but that is no reason for denying the truth given above. All truth has been abused by evil men.

Titus 2:11-15 shows how grace keeps the believer in a walk pleasing to God. In Christianity, grace both saves and teaches, and what an effective teacher it is! It doesn't fill our heads with cold rules, but rather brings our hearts under the subduing influence of the love of God. We learn what pleases God, and having the Holy Spirit, we begin to live the sober, righteous and godly life.

There is a big difference between children kept in order by fear of punishment and those who live in a home where love rules. Order may reign in the former, but it will end in a big explosion when the children grow up. In the latter home, there is both obedience and a joyful response to the parents' desires, the fruit of responsive affection. God rules His children on the love-principle and not on the spanking-principle. May we live our lives in the happy consciousness of this.

∼

Chapter 5

SIN AND SINS

Although there is a close connection between *sin* and *sins,* they are different things. Both are mentioned in Romans 5:12, "Through one man *sin* entered into the world and death through sin; and thus death spread to all men because all *sinned."*

Sin entered the world at the fall of Adam. Just as a snake's poison will run through the whole body from only one bite and do its deadly work, *sin*—the poison of that serpent, the devil—has permeated and ruined man's moral nature. As a result, all have sinned. Thus *sins* of omission or commission in thought, word or act, are chargeable to each of us. *Sin,* then, is the root principle or nature, whereas *sins* are the evil fruits from that evil tree.

We find out what *sin* is in 1 John 3:4, "Whoever commits sin also commits lawlessness, and *sin is lawlessness."* The King James Version (KJV) incorrectly uses the term "transgression of the law" for "sin is lawlessness," but there is a big difference between the two. There can be no transgression of a law unless there is a clear-cut law to disobey, and there was no written law from Adam to Moses. Hence, there was no transgression, and sin wasn't imputed.

Yet sin was there as well as death, sin's penalty (Rom.5:13-14). On the other hand, *lawlessness* is simply the refusal of all rule, the throwing off of divine restraint, the defiance of God's will. Thus Adam began on a *course of sin* when he ate the forbidden fruit.

Instead of being a master, man is now mastered by the evil thing to which he has yielded himself. *Sin* has dominion over him and constantly causes *sins* to be committed. Sin exerts such a deadening influence on the conscience that sinners are unconscious of their terribly dangerous position apart from the grace of God.

When God's grace does act and the Holy Spirit works in life-giving power in a soul, the first cry of that soul is of need and pain. His past sins burden his conscience, and the burden does not end until the value of the precious blood of Christ is known and the person can say, "My sins are forgiven!"

Then, usually at some later time, the question of *sin* is raised with the new believer. We discover that although our *sins* are forgiven, the root principle (sin) from which the sins come, is *still in us*. What is to be done with sin?

It's important to realize that *sin* is the root of our problems. We often get so occupied with the *fruit* (sins) that we forget to consider the *root*. A young man complained to an older Christian that in spite of all his prayers and efforts, he was still constantly sinning. "On what trees do apples grow?" was the only answer he got. "Why, on an apple tree," said the astonished youth. The question seemed so irrelevant.

"And on what trees do plums grow," was the next question. The youth answered, "On a plum tree." The older believer then asked, "On what tree do sins grow?" The youth smiled and answered, "On a sin tree." He then understood that the sins that we Christians commit are not little isolated bits of evil inserted somehow into our lives by Satan. These sins come out as fruit of *sin* which is *within* us. "If we say that we have no *sin*, we deceive ourselves and the truth is not in us" (1 Jn.1:8).

The only remedy for sin is *death!* Death (or the resurrection-change, 1 Cor.15:51-53, if Jesus comes before we die) will end *sin* for us. The last trace will then be gone. We happily anticipate that time!

Do we as joyfully look back to the time when the death of Jesus, the great Remedy, came in? Romans 6:10 says, "For the death that He died, He died to sin once for all, but the life that He lives, He lives to God." He died *for our sins*, atoning for them, but He also died *to sin*. Therefore, as taught by the Holy Spirit, we recognize by faith that we are identified with our great Representative: His death is ours. We, too, then, have "died to *sin*" and we can no longer constantly live in sin (Rom.6:2). Thus, we reckon (consider, count) ourselves "to be dead indeed to sin, but alive to God in Jesus Christ our Lord" (Rom. 6:11).

Notice that the sin to which Jesus died was purely an *external* thing to Himself. "In Him there is no sin" (1 Jn.3:5). *Our* sin is both external and internal. Also, the death of Christ was not only our death to sin, but it was the total condemnation of the sin to which we died. Romans 8:3 says, God "sending His own Son in the likeness of sinful flesh, on account of sin, He *condemned sin in the flesh.*" At the cross, *sin* in its full hideousness, was revealed because lawlessness reached its maximum there, and in that holy sacrifice, its judgment was borne and its condemnation expressed.

Thus *sins* have been borne and their judgment exhausted. *Sin* has been exposed and condemned, and we have died to it in the death of Christ. The cross was all this and more!

In John 1:29 and Romans 8:3, we read of "the sin of the world" and of "sin in the flesh." The first expression is very comprehensive. Sin (the root) and every offshoot of sin in the world is to be taken away by the Lamb of God. He will do it as seen in Revelation 19–21 on the basis of the cross. The second expression, *"sin in the flesh,"* is something different. Sin (the root) is always the same, but the *flesh*—the old, fallen nature of the children of Adam— is the great *vehicle* in which it lives and works to produce *sins* in all individuals.

Imagine a great electrical power network in a city with all the wires without insulation. Fear, shock and death would be everywhere. *Sin* is like the subtle electric current making its influence felt in every direction. The *flesh* is like the generator plus the wires—the seat of the electricity plus the means through which it acts. *Sins* are like the individual shocks which result in death. *The sin of the world* is like the whole power network. But the cross will destroy the whole thing.

We do not find "forgiveness of *sin*" (the root) in the Bible. We *do* find forgiveness of *sins* and of *a* sin. Let's illustrate this. A mother has a son who is rapidly developing a terrible temper. One day, he tries to force his sister to look at something outside the house when she is more

interested in playing with her dolls. In the struggle, he
brings her head with a crash against the window and her
head is cut by the broken glass. His mother sends him to
his room, and when Dad returns, the son is very properly
punished. By evening, the punishment has had its desired
effect. He comes in tears to his parents and confesses his
wrong. They forgive the angry act, but do they forgive the
evil temper from which it sprang? No! If they did, it would
be to condone it. Rather, they strongly condemn it and
lovingly but firmly show the son its evil nature and conse-
quences, and they seek to lead him to hate and condemn it
as much as they do.

"God ... *condemned* sin in the flesh" (Rom.8:3). He did
not condone or forgive it. Now, the work of the Holy Spirit
in us leads us to condemn it just as God has condemned it,
so we may know deliverance from its power.

This does not mean believers won't sin. Condemnation
is not elimination. Sin is still in us (1 Jn.1:8). The Bible
supposes the believer may sin because it gives the divine
provision for such a case (1 Jn.2:1). It even tells us we all
do sin (Jas.3:2).

God has left sin and the flesh (old nature) in the believer
so he can learn their true nature and experimentally come
into line with God's condemnation of them at the cross,
and find life and deliverance in Another. He then can
personally thank God through Jesus Christ that he is delivered (Rom.7:24-25).

First John 3:9 is often thought to conflict with the above
because it says in the KJV and NKJV, "Whosoever is born
of God does not" [commit] "sin." This verse states the

nature of one born of God. But he "does not *practice* sin" is the correct translation of *commit*. It is not the believer's nature to *practice* sin. The apostle John here views believers in their nature as born of God without reference to any abnormal, qualifying features that may occur in the wear-and-tear of life.

What is the effect on a Christian when he sins? It has nothing to do with his *safety* because the cross of Christ is the ground of our safety. There, *sin* was condemned and atonement made, so we are eternally forgiven when we believe. This forgiveness is the *gift* of divine grace and "the gifts and calling of God are irrevocable" (Rom. 11:29). They are not subject to a change of mind on God's part.

However, sins after salvation do reduce the Christian's happiness and remove the joy of both our forgiveness and relationship with God until in self-judgment, such sins are confessed. Then, through the advocacy of Christ, we get the Father's forgiveness (1 Jn.1:9-2:1). We all have to learn painful but profitable lessons in this way and thus discover the true nature of *the flesh* within us and that the only way to keep from gratifying its desires is to "walk in the Spirit" (Gal.5:16).

In closing, let's look a little more at what the Lord Jesus did on the cross in relation to sin. Did He bear the sins of everybody? The Bible says that "He died for all" (2 Cor. 5:15), that He "gave Himself a *ransom* for all" (1 Tim.2:6) and that "He Himself is the propitiation for our sins and not for ours only, but also for" (the sins of) "the whole world" (1 Jn.2:2). These verses show the *Godward* aspect of His work. All are included in its *intention*. So, *propiti-*

ation (God being satisfied) has been made on *behalf* of everyone in the whole world.

When we come to the actual results of His work instead of its intention, things are put differently. We cannot say that He *bore* the sins of everybody because Scripture says, "Who Himself bore *our"* (the believers') "sins" (1 Pet. 2:24) and that "Christ was offered once to bear the sins of *many"* (Heb.9:28). Thank God we are part of the many! [Another has said that Christ was the available Substitute for all, but the *actual* Substitute only for those who believe. Romans 3:22, JND, tells us that the "righteousness of God is ... *towards* all, and *upon* all those who believe." It reaches out to all, but only rests on believers, Ed.].

∽

NOTES

Chapter 6

THE NEW NATURE AND THE OLD

The subject of this chapter meshes closely with what we just had on sin and sins, and both chapters should be studied together.

Many Christians are often conscious of many conflicting desires and emotions. In thought, word and action, they find the strangest possible jumble of good and evil, which is very perplexing to them.

This is cleared up when we realize the believer has two distinct natures, the new and the old. The new nature is the source of every right desire, whereas the old nature is the source of only evil. A hen wouldn't know what to do if made to mother a mixed brood of chicks and ducklings because their natures and consequently their actions are very different. Many Christians are like that hen.

The Lord Jesus told Nicodemus that he had to be born again—"born of water and the Spirit." The Lord then added, "That which is born of the flesh is *flesh*, and that which is born of the Spirit is *spirit*" (Jn.3:5-6). The two words *flesh* and *spirit* plainly indicate the existence of two natures, each characterized by its source. The first is called *flesh* because it springs from the flesh. The other is called *spirit* because it springs from the Holy Spirit.

We can thus speak of the flesh as the *old nature* because we have it as the result of our birth into Adam's race. *Spirit*

is thus the new nature which we get in new birth as born
of the Holy Spirit. However, don't get *spirit*, our new
nature, mixed up with God the Holy Spirit. The new
nature, *spirit*, is the direct result of the Holy Spirit's
wonder-working power, so, although they are closely
connected, the two uses of the word *spirit* are distinct.

When you were born again, the Holy Spirit implanted in
you this new nature and one of the first results was a fight
between it and the old nature. Both natures strive for
mastery, each pulling in opposite directions. Until the
secret of deliverance from the power of the flesh is
learned, the painful jumble of right and wrong will
continue. That painful experience is described for us in
Romans 7. Read it, especially verse 14 to 8:4. Do you see
many of your own experiences there?

Paul reaches one very important conclusion in Romans
7:18. He says, "I know that in me (that is, in my flesh)
nothing good dwells." The flesh is completely bad. God
allows us to wade through the mud of bitter experience so
we may thoroughly learn this vital lesson. The Lord said,
"The flesh profits *nothing*" (Jn.6:63). Paul again states the
same thing in Romans 8:8, "Those who are in the flesh
cannot please God." Only evil can possibly come from the
flesh, our old sinful nature.

*Uncared for and untrained flesh becomes heathen and
savage, whereas educated and refined flesh becomes
restrained, civilized and even religious, but it is still flesh.
That which is born of flesh is flesh, no matter what you do
with it. Absolutely no good thing dwells in even high class
flesh. What can be done with a nature in which sin dwells
and works? What has God done with it? What is His
remedy?*

God answers in Romans 8:3, "For what the law could not do in that it was weak through the flesh, God, did by sending His own Son in the likeness of sinful flesh, on account of sin: He *condemned sin in the flesh.*" The law strongly censured the flesh, but it could neither curb nor even control it so we might be delivered from its power. But in the cross of Christ, God has judicially dealt with it. He "condemned sin in the flesh"—condemned it in the very root of its nature.

Romans 8:4 gives the practical result of this. We have the Holy Spirit to be the power of the new nature, so as we walk in the Spirit, we fulfill all the righteous requirements of the law, although we are no longer under it as our rule of life.

Even though God has condemned our old nature in the cross of Christ, what can *we* do with it? Well, we can thankfully accept what God has done and *treat our old nature as a condemned thing!* We can have absolutely "no confidence in the flesh" (Phil.3:3).

Do we really understand the true character of the flesh, that in it nothing good dwells, and that God has condemned it? Have we reached the point where we have no confidence in it, even in its best forms? This point is not easily reached. Many painful experiences and heart-breaking failures are often passed through as again and again the flesh comes in to damage or wreck our most pious and prayerful resolutions. But once that point is reached, the major battle is just about over.

The shattering of our confidence in the flesh is largely the shattering of the flesh's power over us. This occurs when we look away from ourselves and our most earnest efforts, and find a Deliverer in the Lord Jesus Christ who has taken possession of us by the Holy Spirit. *The Holy Spirit is the power.* He both checkmates the activity of the old nature (Gal.5:16) and energizes, expands and controls the new nature (Rom.8:2,4,5,10) if we allow Him to do so.

It is important to realize the new nature has no power *in itself.* Romans 7 shows us that. The new nature gives us good and beautiful thoughts and desires, *but is powerless to fulfill them. The power comes in complete practical submission to Christ and to the Holy Spirit!* This "walking in the Spirit" largely results from our coming into real agreement with God's condemnation of the old nature in the cross of Christ.

All people, even those who are naturally good natured and even religious, need this new nature. In fact, the man to whom the Lord Jesus said, "You must be born again" (Jn.3:7), was about as good a man as could be found. Morally, socially and religiously, everything was in his favor, yet the Lord said he needed new birth. *Good natured and religious flesh is still only flesh and will not satisfy or please God in any way!*

Thus we see, as far as God is concerned, no one by natural birth has even a spark of good in him. For instance, in Romans 3:9-19, we have a complete account of mankind in his moral features. In verses 10-12, we have sweeping, all-inclusive statements. Then we have the terrible details of some of these features in verses 13-18. In all these words from the God who cannot lie, there is not one word about even a spark of good in mankind, *because that spark is not there!* Scripture is even more positive.

Genesis 6:5 tells us God "saw that the wickedness of man was great in the earth, and that *every* intent of the thoughts of his heart *was only evil continually.*" Paul had learned this truth. In Romans 7:18, he said, "I know that in me (that is, *in my flesh*), *nothing good dwells*"—not even one spark of good!

Remember also that every believer has both the old and the new nature. The old nature is not eradicated at new birth and is not changed by new birth into the new nature. Both natures are in every believer. The process of *grafting* illustrates this. A choice, good and cultivated apple-shoot can be grafted into a wild, useless tree and the tree then can yield good fruit. It is in fact then known by the apple-variety that was grafted in. The same is true with us. Both natures are there, but God only recognizes the new one, so we are "not in the flesh but in the" (Holy) "Spirit" (Rom.8:9).

Further remember that no amount of human effort will avail against our old nature. To have victory over it, we have to think of it and treat it as God does. God entitles you to *disown* the old nature because the new nature is your true self once you are saved, just as the cultivated apple is the recognized nature of the tree as soon as the graft is effective. Your treatment of the old nature is simple. In grafting, the gardener carefully watches his tree if he wants good fruit from it. If the old wild stock seeks to assert itself by throwing up suckers from its roots, the gardener ruthlessly cuts them down as soon as they appear. Likewise, we must quickly and ruthlessly bring the cross of Christ to bear like a sharp knife on our old nature and all of its sinful desires.

Colossians 3:5 tells us to "put to death your members which are on the earth"—cut down the wild suckers. These "suckers" are detailed for us in verses 5, 8 and 9. We are to put them to death in detail. This takes spiritual energy, courage and purpose of heart which you can only have when you willingly look only to the Lord Jesus and place yourself fully in the hands of the Holy Spirit. "If by the" (Holy) "Spirit you put to death the deeds of the body, you will live" (Rom.8:13). [Of course, this does not speak of physical damage to your physical body, but through the Holy Spirit's help, you consider your body as dead to the deeds of the old nature. We see this in Paul's statement in 1 Corinthians 9:27, Ed.].

Thus the Holy Spirit's power is obtained only when we "present yourselves to God as being alive from the dead, and your members as instruments of righteousness to God" (Rom.6:13). Romans 6:19 says to "present your members as slaves of righteousness for holiness." See also Romans 6:22. The thought that such power is obtained by some act of our own will (other than to yield that will to God) is a last desperate attempt to somehow obtain a little bit of credit for the flesh, instead of totally condemning it all, and giving all the glory for victory to God.

The new nature never reaches such perfect growth on earth that a believer will never again sin. An example of this fact is given in 2 Corinthians 12:1-10. Paul had been especially blessed by being caught up into the third heaven, into the presence of God. He had seen and heard things no human language could describe. Then Paul had to resume his ordinary life on earth. From then on, God gave him a "thorn in the flesh"—some infirmity—*so he wouldn't be exalted above measure,* i.e., think too highly of himself because he had been specially privileged. Paul's Christian living was very godly and advanced, but all that was absolutely no insurance against the pride and self-glory which is inherent to the old nature. If Paul was not immune, neither are we.

In closing, let's see how we can distinguish between the desires which come from the old nature and from the new nature. There is no all-inclusive, easy rule. We must continually use the Word of God which is "living and powerful and sharper than any two-edged sword ... and is a discerner of the thoughts and intents of the heart" (Heb.4:12). Then the throne of grace is always available by prayer so we may "find grace to help in time of need" (Heb.4:16). *Thus Bible study and earnest, exercised prayer are absolutely necessary to enable us to untangle and distinguish the thoughts and desires which we find within us!*

However, we can give one general rule. The new nature is *always* true to God; the old nature is *always* true to self. All that truly has Christ as its object is of the new nature, whereas all that has self as its object is of the old nature. Thus, many perplexing questions and problems would be solved by honestly asking, "What is the real (secret) motive which makes me want to do or not do this or that? Is it for Christ-glorification or for self-gratification"?

∾

NOTES

Chapter 7

BLOOD AND WATER

The apostle John was a personal eye-witness to the fact a soldier walked up to the dead Christ hanging on the cross and pierced His side with a spear, and "immediately blood and water came out" (Jn.19:34-35). In 1 John 5:6, John supplemented his previous historical record with the truth of what that event meant spiritually. He said, "This is He who came by water and blood—Jesus Christ; not only by water, but by water and blood." Then in verse 8, he speaks of the Holy Spirit, the water and the blood as the three witnesses to the Son of God.

So we see both blood and water are connected with the *death* of Christ and, although connected, they are sufficiently distinct to be used separately as witnesses. Therefore, we must distinguish them in our thoughts.

Cleansing is connected with both blood and water in Scripture: "The *blood* of Jesus Christ ... cleanses us from all sin" (1 Jn.1:7) and "that He might sanctify and cleanse her" (the true Church) "with the washing of *water* by the Word" (Eph.5:26).

These two cleansings connect themselves with the two great effects of sin, its *guilt* and its *defiling power.* The *blood* sets before us the death of Christ in atonement for our sins, which cancels our guilt and brings us forgiveness. We are thereby cleansed *judicially* (legally). The *water* speaks of the same death, but of its aspect whereby

our sinful state has been judged and ended, to deliver us
from the old conditions and associations of life in which
we once lived. We are thus *morally* cleansed and the
power of sin over us is broken. The hymn writer Toplady
correctly put this thus in the hymn, *Rock of Ages*:

"Let the water and the blood, from Thy riven side which
flowed, Be of sin the double cure, Cleanse me from its
guilt and power."

Hebrews 9 and 10 show us the effectiveness, virtue and
power of the blood of Christ which:

- Purges (cleanses) the sinner's conscience from dead
  works, to serve the living God (9:14).

- Has removed the transgressions of Old Testament
  saints, which transgressions had been accumulating
  under the law (9:15).

- Has ratified a new covenant (contract or testament) of
  grace (9:15-18).

- Has removed the believer's sins and has laid the basis
  for the complete putting away of sin (9:22,26).

- Has so removed the believer's sins for faith, that once
  purged, the believer's conscience is *forever* cleared as
  to the judicial question of his sins (10:2).

- Thus gives the believer boldness to enter into the
  presence of God (10:19).

- Has forever sanctified (set apart) the believer for God
  (10:10,29).

The great subject of Hebrews 9–10 is the believer's access to God as a result of the blood of Christ. The believer is judicially cleared to draw near to God by Christ's one offering, and it *never* needs to be repeated. Hence, the thought of *one* or *once* is repeated seven times in these chapters so we won't overlook the complete sufficiency and great glory connected with the once-spilt precious blood of Christ.

Although judicial (legal) cleansing-by-blood is the great theme in these chapters, *moral cleansing* is not forgotten. We draw near to God with "our hearts sprinkled from an evil conscience and our bodies washed with pure water" (10:22)—evidently an allusion to the consecration of Aaron and his sons to the priestly office (Ex.29). They were washed with water (v.4) and also sprinkled with blood (v.20), all picturing the death of Christ. Thus, Christ's *blood* judicially cleanses us and gives us a perfect standing before God, while the *water* cleanses us morally by cutting us off from the old life in which we once lived and bringing us into the new life.

The moral cleansing by water needs to be kept up. Aaron and his sons were bathed with water from head to toe at their consecration, and that bathing was not repeated. However, a laver was provided (Ex.30:17-21) where the priests were instructed to wash their hands and feet. "When they go into the tabernacle of meeting ... they shall wash with water *lest they die.*"

Just before He instituted His supper, the Lord Jesus girded Himself, poured water into a basin and began to wash His disciples' feet (Jn.13). Peter's reluctance to let Jesus do it was used by the Lord to bring forth the truth

that such washing is necessary if *communion* with the
Lord in His heavenly position was to be enjoyed. He told
Peter, "If I do not wash you, you have no part *with* Me"
(v.8). Peter's rapid change from reluctance to over-enthu-
siasm led the Lord to say, "He who is bathed needs only to
wash his feet, but is completely clean" (v.10).

This verse clearly distinguishes our two-fold cleansing
by water. All we believers have been bathed (washed all
over) once-for-all by the death of Christ: it *has* cleansed us
from the old life. However, we also need the *daily appli-
cation* of that death to our souls. We cannot enjoy "part
with Christ" without it.

Thus the coming of Jesus Christ, the Son of God, was
characterized by *both* water and blood. As we saw in
1 John 5:6, the Holy Spirit especially guards this point by
saying, "not only by water, but by water and blood." Why?
Perhaps one reason is the tendency to forget the blood—to
say Christ came to simply cleanse man morally by setting
him high ideals and then living out those ideals as an
incentive for others to live a good life. Such people say He
thus makes "atonement"—"at-one-ment"—and brought
man and God together as one on the basis of good living.
To counteract this false teaching, the Holy Spirit empha-
sizes both the moral cleansing and expiation (payment) for
sin!

So the three witnesses (the Spirit, water and blood) to
the Son of God remain. The Holy Spirit is the living,
acting and speaking Witness, while the water and the
blood are the two silent witnesses, but all three testify that
He who came in this manner is the Son of God, the
Fountain of eternal life; and for us who believe, this

eternal life is ours in Him (1 Jn.5:5-13). May we truly thank God that both blood and water flowed from that spear wound!

No blood and water flowed from Christ during His life. Consequently, contrary to what some believe, Christ's *life*, as wonderful as it was, had no part in His payment for our sins. Sometimes Romans 5:19 is used to teach otherwise. It says, "By one Man's obedience many will be made righteous." However, a careful reading of the context (vv.12-21) shows the opposite.

The two heads of their races, Adam and Christ, are being contrasted here, with the sin of one (Adam) with its subsequent disaster, and the righteousness and obedience of the Other (Christ), with its subsequent blessing. It is a question of the "one offense" and the "one righteousness" (v.18, JND). Christ's one righteousness was obedience *"even unto death and that the death of the cross"* (Phil. 2:8, JND).

Since the blood cleanses us from all sin, why do we need the water? That question is best answered by another question: "Are you not conscious of as much need for cleansing from the *love* of sin as from the *condemnation* of sin?" Christians need to *hate* sin. That is the reason for the water. We also need the daily cleansing of which the laver speaks. There is much concerning us personally, as well as many subtle influences of this world, that need to be removed.

We don't go back to the blood for daily cleansing. The believer is not to continually, so to speak, go through the cleansing and justifying process as to eternal salvation from sin, of which the blood speaks. "By one offering, He has perfected *forever* those who are ... sanctified" (Heb. 10:14). However, some have felt that 1 John 1:7, "The blood of Jesus Christ, His Son, cleanses us from all sin," instructs us to go to the blood for daily cleansing. The word *cleanses* in this verse simply points out the inherent property of Christ's precious blood, that it will *always* cleanse every sinner who comes by faith to Christ for salvation.

We often use the present tense in this way. We say that "fire burns wood." We don't mean that the fire will burn the wood a little bit almost every day (the wood can be burned up only once), but that an inherent, well-known property of fire is that it burns wood. Thus 1 John 1:7 does not support daily cleansing by blood.

Since Scripture does speak of our daily washing or cleansing *by water,* how do we get washed? *It is by the Word of God, our Bibles.* The water and the Word of God are clearly connected by Ephesians 5:26, "that He might sanctify and cleanse her" (the Church) "with the washing of water *by the Word.*" The Word alone shows us the wonderful death of Christ. Sin is thereby also clearly revealed. Our affections are thus cleansed. In Psalm 119:9, the question is asked as to how shall a young man cleanse his ways. The answer is, "By taking heed according to Your Word."

We often overlook this cleansing effect of God's Word even when we are anxious to study our Bibles. A young believer once told of the problem she had of remembering the teaching which she had heard. An older believer told her to go and bring him a sieve full of water, but each time she tried, all the water ran through the sieve. When she finally told him he had asked her to do an impossible thing, he pointed out that even if one drop of water hadn't been retained, *the sieve was much cleaner than before.* Let us dwell often on God's Word! Even if we don't become great Bible scholars, our lives will be cleansed thereby.

In John 3:5 we read about being *born of water.* By the water of the Word applied in the power of the Holy Spirit we are born again—made to possess a new life and a new nature which includes the condemnation of the old life and nature. As we have seen, this is pictured by the *bathing* of the priests from head to foot (Ex.29:4; Jn.13:10). John 3:5 doesn't speak of baptism!

The Lord only speaks of one new birth, which is by water and the Holy Spirit—the water being the instrument and the Holy Spirit being the power. This new birth is declared by the Lord to be indefinable and not controlled by man (3:8). Water baptism is both definable and completely controlled by man, so John 3:5 obviously does not speak of it.

In summary, we need the water both when we sin and (even if not sinning) while we are in this world of defilement, if we would worship, have communion (fellowship) with, or serve God. In Numbers 19, water is pictured as that which purifies from sin. In Exodus 30:17-21, water is pictured as removing every earthly defilement (without reference to any actual sins) so we can draw near to God. We have also looked at this last aspect in the feet-washing in John 13. We also need the blood given once for all.

∽

NOTES

Chapter 8
GRACE AND DISCIPLESHIP

The very essence of the grace of God is that it is free and unconditional. The conditions for its *reception* are repentance and faith, but grace itself is unhampered by any condition. Some people give with one hand and take away with the other, or add in so many restrictions and conditions that the gift is useless to the recipient, but this is not God's way.

Yet Luke 9:23 tells us that "if anyone desires to come after Me, let him deny himself and take up his cross daily and follow Me." Why the "if"? What does it mean? Is salvation really free, or must we make a bargain for it with the Lord? How about other verses that contain similar "ifs"?

In answer, read Luke 14:25-35. Verse 26 says, "If anyone comes to Me and does not hate his father and mother, wife and children, brothers and sisters, yes and his own life also, *he cannot be My disciple."* Those four last words are repeated three times (vv.26,27,33). Note they don't say anything about *salvation*, but rather, about being the Lord's *disciple!*

The preceding paragraph (Lk.14:15-24) contains the parable of the *great supper* which is a marvelous unfolding of the grace of God. Thus, having just explained divine grace in a manner that brought great crowds about Him, the Lord Jesus then tests their reality by giving them the terms of *discipleship.*

Although grace and discipleship are two different things, they must be looked at together and in their proper order. *Grace* is a special form or character of divine love—its character when it stoops to go forth to the completely undeserving and adapts to their needs (although far surpassing those needs).

On the other hand, *discipleship* is a special form or character of a *believer's* love which comes from a response to God's love. It is the reverse or backwards flow of divine love to its Source. A *disciple* is both a *learner* and a *follower.* When the grace of God grasps a soul and new life begins, its first instincts are to learn about and from the Savior and to follow Him. Thus loving grace is the source and power of discipleship.

In the parable of the great supper mentioned above, we find the door of salvation swung wide open and the very worst people invited. No demand, condition or bargain is made on them. Grace is not hindered or dimmed by such things. Yet the Lord was well aware of two things when He spoke this parable:

1. Many would only *profess* to have received grace. There would be no reality.

2. Those who really received grace have thereby received a responsive love in their souls that draws them irresistibly after the One from whom it comes, and those people desire to learn what is pleasing to Him.

This is why the Lord followed up His declaration of grace with instruction as to discipleship, and then added two short parables to show the importance of *counting the cost of discipleship* (Lk.14:28-33).

One day, a sad looking man told me, "It costs too much to be a Christian." Was he right? If he meant it costs too much to be saved, he was wrong because salvation costs us nothing. That incredible cost has fallen on the One who was able to bear it and He, being made sin for us, *has* borne it all.

If the man meant it costs too much to be a *disciple,* he was wrong again! It *costs* to be a disciple, but it doesn't cost *too much!* The fact is that the sad-looking man was not saved. He had never tasted grace, so he had nothing to spend. When a man goes shopping with no money in his pocket, *everything* costs too much! The man was putting demand before supply, the cart before the horse.

Discipleship costs constant sacrifice on our part. We must work to strengthen our Christian position and expend considerable energy in fighting our enemies.

The first parable on counting the cost (Lk.14:28-30) speaks of work. "Which of you, intending to build a tower...." If you want to follow the Lord, you must build a tower. A tower speaks of *protection.* We are kept by the power of God through faith (1 Pet.1:5). We are responsible to build up ourselves on our most holy faith.

Therefore, "praying in the Holy Spirit" is our only proper attitude, and the result is to keep ourselves "in the love of God" (Jude 20-21). We are well protected when the love of God surrounds us as our tower of defense. Faith builds. "The faith" as found in the Word of God is the strong foundation on which we build, and prayer is the attitude best suited to such building. Thus, the love of God, *consciously known,* is our tower of defense.

All this is only a means to an end. We become strong *defensively* so we can act *offensively* against the enemy. We see this in the second parable (vv.31-33): "Or what king going to make war ...." A disciple should move offensively, positively, aggressively. Notice that king proposed to take the offensive against another king with twice as large an army. That's a bold move! But behind his back, he was well fortified: his tower was built. This is God's way! For instance, David's tower had been built in his wilderness experiences of meeting and killing a lion and a bear. Therefore, the giant *Goliath* didn't scare him.

Discipleship means all this. It means earnest prayer and earnest Bible study. It means deep exercise and the shock of battling the world, the flesh and the devil. Sit down and count the cost! Does it scare you? If so, then recount the cost in the full light of the power of God and the riches of grace, and you will begin to "rejoice in Christ Jesus" and even more deeply have "no confidence in the flesh."

Thus grace and discipleship go hand in hand as seen by the case of blind Bartimaeus (Mk.10:46-52). Grace in the Person of the Lord Jesus stood still at his cry for help and freely gave him all he desired. "Jesus said to him, Go your way," i.e. "Go where you want: no terms are imposed on you." But where did Bartimaeus go? "Immediately he received his sight *and followed Jesus on the road (*or, *in the way).*" Impelled by grace, he entered the path of discipleship. *He followed Jesus* (v.52).

Discipleship does not belong to only a few—a clergy. There are no favored-ones in Christianity. All the early Christians were believers and saints and disciples (Acts 1:15; 6:1; 9:38; 19:9; 20:7). Even Paul was a believer, a saint and a disciple along with the rest, although he was gifted directly from heaven and given authority.

Unfortunately, the world has conquered much of the Christian profession. The unscriptural clergy-laity system is everywhere. However, the true Christianity of the Bible knows nothing of these things. Shame on us if we receive our spiritual sight and then, unlike Bartimaeus, go strolling off to amuse ourselves with the novel sights of Jericho! Yet there is a constant tendency in that direction. Therefore, the Lord said to some believers, "If you *abide* in My Word, you are My disciples indeed" (Jn.8:31). Discipleship belongs to all Christians, but there are many believers who are not "disciples indeed"—real, earnest followers of the Lord Jesus.

Let's again look at the *conditions* for Christian discipleship in Luke 14:25-33. The whole thing comes down to the necessity of *putting Christ first* and all else in last place. In a comparative sense, we are to hate all else. Our love to Christ should be so strong compared to our natural love for our relations, that the latter appears as hate (Lk.14:26). See Luke 9:59-60 for an example of this.

Likewise, in Luke 14:33, we are told to *forsake* all we have. Our affections are to be severed from our possessions because they now belong to our Master and thus are to be held for Him. This *may* mean giving up everything as did the early Christians, or like Levi (Lk.5:27-29), we may "leave all" and yet still have possessions. Levi's house still belonged to him, but it and his money were used for the Lord, to make a great feast for Christ and draw sinners to Him. This is an important example for us!

If Christ is to be first, *self* must go, so the disciple must *deny himself* and take up His cross daily (Lk.9:23-26). We must *inwardly* say "No" to self. We must be as a dead man as far as the working of our will is concerned. Then, *outwardly,* we must take up His cross daily. We must accept *death* as cutting us off from the world and its glory. We must say "No" to the love of reputation and popularity. All this is hard work, bitter to the flesh, but it is sweetened by the love of Christ! These are the conditions for discipleship. See also Luke 9:46-62.

Discipleship today means exactly the same thing as it did 2000 years ago. There are some minor details that are different because we live in different times, but it still means saying "No" to our own wills. It still means the cross: the world will hate us. In early times (and still in some parts of the world), this hatred was manifested by sword, cross, wild beasts or flame. Now it is usually by silent contempt, a well-timed snub or social exclusion. The early attacks were often swift and severe, and it was all over; for us, the attack tends to be *chronic*—mild but long-lasting.

Discipleship still means walking in the spirit of self-judgment and separation from the world in even its religious forms. It means giving up anything questionable or stumbling to others for His Name's sake, even things *lawful* in themselves, because our question must constantly be, "What does *He* want?"

Obviously, a true disciple will lose much in this world. But he gains "many times more in this present time and in the age to come, eternal life" (Lk.18:30). The gain will not be in what appeals to the natural man: it will be a higher (spiritual) gain. "If anyone serves Me, let him follow Me; and where I am, there My servant will be also. If anyone serves Me, him My Father will honor" (Jn.12:26). *The gain will be companionship with Christ and honor from the Father!* Who can count such wonderful gain!

After having been told of discipleship, three disciples got a glimpse of such gain when they witnessed the transfiguration (Lk.9:27-36). They were "with Him on the holy mount" (2 Pet.1:16-18). Thus Paul, who lost all for Christ, dismissed the loss-side of discipleship as "our light affliction" and proclaimed the gain or profit-side as *"a far more exceeding and eternal weight of glory"* (2 Cor.4:17-18).

One more distinction in terms. Paul was an apostle, but he was also a disciple. The two things are clearly different as shown by Luke 6:13, "He" (Jesus) "called His disciples to Himself; and from them, He chose twelve whom He also named apostles." The word *disciple* means one *taught or trained.* The word *apostle* means one *sent forth.* Every true follower of the Lord was a disciple, but only the twelve sent forth by the Lord (plus several others later, including Paul) were apostles. Theirs was a unique place of authority and service. They were involved with the *foundation* of the Church (Eph.2:20) and have long since passed away, but millions of the Lord's disciples are to be found even today.

The *power* for discipleship is found only in God, but it reaches us in a simple way. There is an *impulsive* (explosive, motivating, pushing) power in *affection*. When the love of God enters even the darkest heart, a new impelling power is known and discipleship begins. The power that starts discipleship also sustains it. Read John 14–16 which is a manual for discipleship. You will find *love* is the source for everything. The Holy Spirit is the power, and *obedience* (obeying Christ's commandments) is the pathway into which the Spirit leads the disciple.

In seeking to live as disciples of the Lord Jesus, you will need three things. *First,* you will need spiritual wisdom and discretion (proper judgment) which only comes from the Scriptures wherein we find the Lord's will for us. Our business as disciples is (with the Holy Spirit's help) to search out that will. This means we must be very familiar with our Bibles and carefully study them.

Prayer is the *second* thing. We must maintain a spirit of dependence on God which comes through prayer. Thirdly, we must always seek to be *obedient*. As disciples, our business is to obey, not to do some great thing which we think the Lord would like. Therefore, let us lay aside every "weight" that would hinder us (Heb.12:1) and remember our Master's words, "If you know these things, blessed are you if you do them" (Jn.13:17).

∼

Chapter 9

ELECTION AND FREE GRACE

From the beginning of Scripture history, two great facts form the basis of all of God's dealings with men. The first is that God is absolutely sovereign. The second is that man is an intelligent creature with moral faculties and is thus responsible to his Creator.

To some people, there is a contradiction between the sovereignty of God expressing itself in the election of some for blessing and the free offer of grace to all. The hyper-Calvinists solve the difficulty by discarding man's responsibility, while the Arminians solve the difficulty by discarding God's sovereignty. But both of these "solutions" are unscriptural since they deny the above scriptural facts. The real difficulty is that our little minds have difficulty in grasping God's great thoughts.

The first fact is seen in Genesis 1:1, "In the beginning God created the heaven and the earth." God is sovereign. Then God created man "in Our image, according to our likeness" and gave man dominion (Gen.1:26). Here we see man made as God's representative in creation. He was originally a free, intelligent, moral agent, fully responsible for his actions. Although man is no longer sinless but fallen, his responsibility remains.

One of the greatest confessions of God's sovereignty came from Nebuchadnezzar, the great Gentile king in whom *human* sovereignty reached its highest expression.

He said, [God] "does according to His will in the army of
heaven. And among the inhabitants of the earth, no one
can restrain His hand or say unto Him, 'What have You
done?'" (Dan.4:35). On the other hand, the responsibility
of man in his fallen state is clearly shown in Romans 1:18-
3:19 where Paul shows the complete ruin of mankind. If
sin destroyed a person's responsibility, there would be
every excuse for man's ruined condition, but Paul shows
the most degraded heathen, the most refined idolater and
the very religious Jew are equally "without excuse."

Believers are addressed as *chosen* "in Him" (Christ)
"before the foundation of the world" (Eph.1:4) and as
"elect according to the foreknowledge of God the Father"
(1 Pet.1:2). The Lord told His disciples that "you did not
choose Me, but I chose you" (Jn.15:16) and that "no one
can come to Me unless the Father who has sent Me, draws
him" (Jn.6:44).

Shall we then reason from these scriptures that all
gospel efforts are useless; that to preach to any except
those chosen of God is a waste of time? Let's look at what
the apostles did. Peter in Acts 2:40 *urged* his hearers,
when pricked in their hearts, to "Be saved from this
perverse generation." In Acts 3:19, he told rebellious
sinners to "repent ... and be converted." Paul preached
"repentance toward God and faith toward our Lord Jesus
Christ" (Acts 20:21).

Shouldn't the apostles have rather said, "You can do
absolutely nothing. You are spiritually dead and therefore
you must simply await the pleasure of God. If He has
elected you, you will be saved; if not, you will be lost." Or
should the apostles have said, "Man is an absolutely free

agent and is capable of choosing the right way if it is put before him in a sufficiently attractive manner. God knows the end from the beginning, but He has no particular will regarding anybody. Therefore, we must do all we can to make the gospel attractive to win men." However, the apostles didn't say these things. The fact is, if we incline to either set of scriptures in the previous paragraph at the expense of the other, we will be exposing ourselves to the Lord's words in Luke 24:25, "O foolish ones and slow of heart to believe in all that the prophets have spoken."

All the above difficulties will vanish once we clearly see the true character of man's ruin and of God's grace. By sinning, man has placed himself under a burden of guilt and has made himself liable for judgment. He has also become possessed by a completely evil fallen nature and has a heart (an inner self) that is "deceitful above all things and *desperately wicked"* (Jer.17:9).

Further, sin has acted like a subtle drug that has so stupefied and perverted man's reason, will and judgment that "there is *none* who understands, there is *none* who seeks after God" (Rom.3:11). Even in the wonderful presence of grace and the sweet pleadings of the gospel, men reject the One who wants to save them and prefer the empty and short-lived follies of the world. Like a "herd of many swine" (Mt.8:31-32), they rush to destruction. Thus, their only hope is the *sovereign intervention of God.*

The parable of the "great supper" in Luke 14:15-24 illustrates this. The well-laden supper table represents the spiritual blessings resulting from the death of Christ at great cost. All is ready and yet no one comes. Something else is needed: *the mission of the Holy Spirit,* pictured by the errand of the servant. The house was filled *only because He compelled (forced) people to come in.* Therefore, once we realize the full extent of our ruin as a result of sin, we will realize the sovereign action of God in choosing us and drawing us to Himself by the compelling-power of the Holy Spirit was our only hope. Instead of quarreling with this side of the truth, it will bow our hearts in grateful worship before Him.

However, poor, fallen, self-destroyed man is still a responsible creature. His reason, will and judgment are perverted, but not destroyed. Hence, the largeness of the grace of God. What is grace? Is it God's goodness which saves the elect? No, that is *mercy.* In Romans 9 and 11, where election is the great subject, *mercy* is mentioned again and again. *Rather, grace is the mighty outflow of the heart of God toward the utterly sinful and undeserving.* It shows no partiality and knows no restrictions. It includes "all men" (1 Tim.2:3-6) and "where sin abounded, grace abounded much more" (Rom.5:20).

We see *grace* in the last great commission of the risen Christ to His disciples, "that repentance and remission of sins should be preached in His name to all nations, beginning at Jerusalem" (Lk.24:47). These instructions were similar to those given by the king in the parable of the feast in Matthew 22:1-14, "Go into the highways and as many as you find, invite to the wedding."

In this parable we have *servants*, not "the Servant" as in Luke 14. The *servants* are not the Holy Spirit in His sovereign and secret activities, but saved men who simply do the King's business. They give the invitation to all whom they find, without raising questions as to their character or as to whether the people are chosen or not. All who listen are gathered in, both bad and good in the eyes of men, and the wedding is "filled with guests."

Knowing it pleases God "through the foolishness of the message preached to save those who believe" (1 Cor. 1:21), the evangelist proclaims the gospel far and wide. When men believe his message, he gives all the credit to the Holy Spirit and rejoices over them, knowing their election of God (1 Th.1:4).

There is nothing in the truth of *election* to stumble the seeking sinner [although election is a truth for believers to enjoy, not something to be preached to the unsaved, Ed.]. The very fact that he is seeking, indicates he is being drawn by the Father. The idea that a sinner may be desperately seeking for the Savior in this day of grace and yet not be heard (and consequently eternally lost), because he isn't elected, is a terrible distortion of the truth.

The Lord's words are "Seek and you will find" (Mt.7:7). In fact, election has nothing to do with the sinner as such. It is never used in the Bible in any gospel preaching, although it is frequently mentioned to establish the faith of *believers*. Election generally only causes difficulty for the unsaved when unbalanced preachers take it from its proper scriptural setting and thrust it on their unsaved hearers.

We are "elect according to the foreknowledge of God the Father" (1 Pet.1:2). Election is then distinct from God's foreknowledge, but is based on it. God's election or choice is not a blind, fatalistic casting of the lot. That is a purely heathen thought. God chooses in the full light of His foreknowledge. Hence, no sinner who really *wants* to be saved will ever find the door shut because he is not one of the elect. In fact, his very *desire* is the fruit of the Holy Spirit's work. Also, God's choice (as with Jacob and Esau) is *always* justified by results (compare Romans 9:12-13 with Malachi 1:2-3).

[Note: We are never told what it is in the divine foreknowledge that determines our election. However, it was *not* based on divine foreknowledge of *our* faith or merit, because that would mean our salvation was based on our own works and not on grace alone (Rom.9:11; Eph.2:8-9 and 2 Tim.1:9). In fact, we can't even boast of having faith when someone else doesn't, because *even our faith was God's gift to us:* "For by grace you have been saved through faith, *and that" (faith) "not of yourselves; it is the gift of God, not of works,* lest anyone should boast" (Eph. 2:8-9) Ed.].

We are never told why God didn't simply elect everybody. Would our little minds be able to even grasp His reasons if He had chosen to explain His infinite ways to us? But we may be sure that all of God's ways are in perfect harmony with the facts that "God is light" and "God is love" (1 Jn.1:5; 4:8). If men still want to argue, we will have to be content with the Scripture that says, "Look ... I will answer you. For God is greater than man. Why do you contend with Him? For He does not give an accounting of any of His words" (Job 33:12-13). After all, being God, *why should He?* Read also Romans 9:14-24.

Some wonder how man can be held responsible when he is so incapable of choosing right. Using the example of the poor woman arrested for the 201st time for being drunk and disorderly, the plea was that since she was so

degraded as to be incapable of resisting alcohol or choosing a better life, she was no longer responsible in any way.
But her plea did not avail. No sane person believes that
one has only to sink low enough into crime to be freed
from responsibility and punishment. By sin, man has
plunged himself into immeasurable perversity and inca-
pacity, but his responsibility remains.

Free grace means that the *intentions* of God's gospel
embrace all, not that our salvation is simply our choice by
our own so-called free will. Christ died for all (1 Tim.2:4-
6) and the gospel is sent freely to all—just as freely as if
all received it, even though most reject it. However, multitudes *do* receive it and then the righteousness of God
which is "to all" in its intention, is "on all who believe" in
its actual effect (Rom.3:22-24, NKJV, KJV, JND). Such
are saved by grace through faith, which is not of themselves, but is the gift of God (Eph.2:8-9). Their blessing is
from God from first to last, and they should regard themselves as chosen of Him.

The sinner has to *receive,* not *choose* Christ. *Choose* is
an active word which implies certain powers of discrimi-
nation and personal selection, *which powers the sinner
does not have. Receive* is a passive word which indicates
the sinner simply falls into line with God's offer. "As
many as *received"* Christ (Jn.1:12) are saved, and this
receiving was the result of God's gracious working in new
birth (Jn.1:13), not of any so-called *free will* which man no
longer has.

Yet it is proper to *urge* sinners to repent and believe.
Our Lord did so in Mark 1:15 and so did Peter in Acts
3:19, and Paul in Acts 16:31; 20:21 and 26:20. We should

proclaim that *faith* is the principle on which God justifies
the sinner and also *urge* men to believe. The fact that faith
is only the result of God's work in the soul and all spiritual enlargement for the believer is only through the work
of the Holy Spirit, in no way is against God's servants
earnestly persuading men. Paul preached "with much
earnest striving" (1 Th.2:2, JND) and speaks of *"persuading* men" (2 Cor.5:11). These examples show God's will,
regardless of any arguments to the contrary.

Some sinner may give you the excuse that he can't
believe until God gives him the power. However, both
repentance and faith require *weakness* rather than power.
To *repent* is to own the truth as to yourself; to *believe* is to
lean your poor shattered soul on Christ. God's command
is *man's enabling* as seen by the man with the withered
hand in Luke 6:6-10. The power to stretch it out was there
the instant Christ spoke the words. If the sinner is *anxious*
to believe, God will give him the ability, because if there
is the smallest desire towards Christ in a sinner's heart,
grace will bring it to definite faith and salvation. See
Philippians 1:6.

The above remark would probably come from one who
simply wanted to argue, in which case we would have to
leave (ignore) him. However, if the person was really
anxious and perplexed, I would urge him to rest with
simple confidence in the Savior and to believe those great
truths which are so plain that "whoever walks the road,
although a fool, shall not go astray" (Isa.35:8).

I would also urge him to not occupy himself with questions about God's sovereignty, which he cannot understand. *Never allow what you don't know to disturb what*

you do know! Never forget that the Christ who said, "All whom the Father gives Me will come to Me," immediately added, "and the one who comes to Me, I will by no means cast out" (Jn.6:37).

~

NOTES

Chapter 10

ISRAEL AND THE CHURCH

One must have a knowledge of *dispensational truth* to properly understand the Bible. God has dealt with people in different ways at various times and brought in fresh revelations of Himself and of His will. Dispensational truth teaches us to rightly distinguish these different ways and to discern their nature, so the outstanding features of each dispensation will be understood. We thus learn the true character of our calling and of our dispensation.

The prominent feature of the previous dispensation was *Israel,* God's chosen earthly people. Our present dispensation began on the day of Pentecost (50 days after Christ's resurrection) and is marked by completely different features: the *Church,* not Israel, is prominent in God's thoughts.

We do not mean the *Jews* when we speak of *Israel.* We mean what that nation was in God's *original* plan for them. In like manner, by the Church, we do not mean any building or denomination or group of professed believers banded together at some location, but simply *all those* called out of the world to God by Himself during this dispensation of Christ's rejection.Thus, we speak of the Church according to God's original design and thoughts. The Greek word translated *church* in most Bible translations simply means *called out ones.* So by God's calling and the indwelling Holy Spirit, all believers are banded together into God's Assembly or Church.

The word *church* (ecclesia: called-out ones) is used in three ways in Scripture: to denote the total number of Christians in any given place (1 Cor.1:2; Col.4:15); the total number of Christians on earth at any particular time (1 Cor.10:32; 12:28; Eph.1:22); and the total number of Christians (called out and sealed by the Holy Spirit) between Pentecost and the *Rapture*, the Lord's coming to the air (Eph.3:21; 5:25). We will generally use the word in its last (universal) usage, although if we speak of the Church as it exists on earth today, we obviously mean the previous usage where the Church is like an army which remains the same even though the units that compose it are changing in both number and personnel.

Having defined our terms, let's observe some distinctions. John the Baptist, the forerunner of Christ, was the last of a long line of prophets of the previous dispensation. God's utterances under the old dispensation stopped with him. "The law and the prophets were until John. Since that time, the kingdom of God has been preached" (Lk.16:16).

The coming of Christ into the world was described by Zacharias as the coming of the Dayspring *(sun rising)* from on high (Lk.1:78). His appearance on earth proclaimed the dawn of a new day—not its actual beginning as yet. The Lord Jesus had a mission to fulfill in the midst of Israel, so He needed to present Himself to them as their long-promised Messiah.

Moreover, the foundations for blessing must be laid amid the sufferings of Calvary. But when all this was past, when the Lord Jesus had died, risen again, ascended to heaven and sent down the Holy Spirit, *then* the new day (dispensation) began. It was indeed new: it was completely different from all that had gone before.

The characteristic feature of the old dispensation was *law,* whereas *grace* is the main feature of the new dispensation. The old dispensation began with the giving of the *Law* at Sinai. Under the law, God *demanded* from men. God was to receive His due from men. The fact that man immediately and completely failed did not in any way relieve men of their new responsibilities. However, God told Moses that in *mercy,* He would withhold the threatened destruction in view of the coming of Christ (Ex. 33:19). The law, however, continued to be a *schoolmaster* or *tutor* (Gal.3:24) until Christ came.

In time, Christ came. A Power stronger than the law was present in Him, as seen in the case of the sinful woman in John 8:1-11. Under the potent influence of grace, the hypocrites were convicted far more effectively than under law. Further, the sinner was forgiven; something the law could not do. Thus, today, God gives and man receives. The new dispensation is thus marked by grace that "reigns through righteousness to eternal life through Jesus Christ our Lord" (Rom.5:21).

The old dispensation centered around Israel, whereas the new is connected with the Church. The law was only given to Israel, so God's attention was focused on Israel as a nation. Their privileges were national, not individual, although God always had His secret dealings with individuals and these dealings were more prominent in the days of national failure. But at their beginning, God took them up nationally without reference to the spiritual state of individuals: Israel's standing before Him was on a national basis.

On the other hand, there is nothing national about the Church. Today, God visits *all nations* "to take out of them a people for His name" (Acts 15:13-14). Those thus gathered out for His name comprise the Church. The Church is thus extra-national, not national or even international. It is completely outside of all national distinctions and totally independent of such. The Church is *one flock* (Jn.10:16), *one body* (1 Cor.12:13), a *spiritual house, a holy priesthood* (1 Pet.2:5), and *a family* comprised of the children of God (1 Jn.2:12; 3:1).

Moreover, the Church is comprised of *individuals* who have personally been made right with God, are forgiven and are indwelt by the Holy Spirit. Only then do they become members of the body and "living stones" (1 Pet.2:5) in the spiritual house.

A ritualistic worship was connected with Israel—a worship that only pictured the future workings of God. The Church's privileges are connected with the eternal realities themselves—with substance rather than shadows. The Church's worship does not consist of sacrificial offerings and symbolic ceremonies, but of "worship in spirit and truth" (Jn.4:23-24). The law (Judaism) had only a "shadow of the good things to come, and not the very image of the things" (Heb.10:1). But for us, the good things have come. Christ has established them (Heb.9:24; 10:12), the Holy Spirit has revealed them (1 Cor.2:9-10) and the believer may gaze on them with the eye of faith (2 Cor.4:18).

Israel's blessings were mainly earthly and material, whereas the Church's are heavenly and spiritual. Israel was instructed to thank God when they finally possessed their promised land by taking the first of all their crops and placing them in a basket before the Lord, with an acknowledgment of His goodness on their lips (Dt.26:1-11).

But the Christian's approach to God is far from this materialistic way. Our heavenly inheritance is spoken of thus: "Blessed be the God and Father of our Lord Jesus Christ, *who has blessed us with every spiritual blessing in the heavenly places" [heavenlies] "in Christ"* (Eph.1:3). How complete a contrast!

Israel's destiny is to be the channel of blessing to all nations during the Lord's future 1000-year reign (Isa.60). The Church's destiny is association with Christ in heaven (Rev.19, 21), showing the Church as the Lamb's wife.

Although the death of Christ marked the close of God's dealings with Israel *as a nation* (they showed their utter hatred of God), God nevertheless continued certain supplementary dealings with Israel until the death of Stephen (Acts 7:54-60) and perhaps even to the destruction of Jerusalem in AD 70. Likewise, although our present dispensation (and the Church itself) began on the day of Pentecost, God *gradually* revealed His plans for His Church over many years, particularly through the apostle Paul.

Also, we should note God's ways with Israel have only ended *for a time.* In the future, all the glorious promises made to that favored nation will be fulfilled. Israel has simply been put on a taxiway while the Church occupies the main runway. When the Church is transferred to heaven, Israel will again be brought out on the main line of God's dealings.

In Acts 7:38, KJV, Stephen speaks of "the church in the wilderness" and the headings of many Old Testament chapters in the KJV also speak of the church. Thus, many believe the Church existed in Old Testament times. Israel *was* the "assembly" or "congregation" in the wilderness, just as the unruly mob of Diana's worshipers were called an "assembly" in Acts 19:41, but these can in no way be connected to *the* Church of the New Testament.

Further, the chapter headings in the KJV are not inspired, and thus to apply certain prophetic utterances to the Church is simply the mistaken views of well-meaning men. However, the mistake is a serious one because this confusion of Israel with the Church has been used by people to bring Jewish principles and ceremonies into Christianity.

Men like Abraham, Moses and Elijah were thus never part of the Church: they were of the past dispensation. Morally, these men were giants, while many of us believers are only pygmies. God will bless them for their godliness, *but not as part of the Church*. Even John the Baptist, than whom none was greater, was, when viewed dispensationally, less than the least in the kingdom of heaven (Mt.11:11). He belonged to the dispensation of servitude; we to the dispensation of *sonship* (Gal.4:1-7).

While on earth, the Lord Jesus pronounced a new thing, a future work, of which these great men of old had no part. On *Himself,* the Rock, He said "I *will build* My Church" (Mt.16:18). It was to be founded on the Son of the living God, not on a mere prophet, no matter how great. This is *our* portion!

Israel was called to take possession of the Promised Land for God as a pledge that the whole earth belonged to Him, even though Satan had usurped dominion over it. When Israel entered the Land, they crossed the Jordan River as the people of "the Lord of all the earth" (Josh.3:11-13). Further, their calling was to preserve in the world the people "from whom, according to the flesh, Christ came" (Rom.9:4-5).

Also God used Israel as the final proof of the utter depravity of man. Israel was separated from all the surrounding corruptions and privileged beyond all others, yet, as shown in the records of their own law (Rom.3:9-18), they completely failed and proved in this way the hopelessly fallen condition of all. If, as Romans 3:19 puts it, the law completely condemns even the specially treated and blessed nation of the Jews who were under the law, then *every* mouth is stopped and *all the world* is "guilty before God."

On the other hand, God's object and purpose with the Church is that *He* is to be expressed in it. It is Christ's body (Eph.1:23). We live and express ourselves in our physical bodies; so Christ lives and expresses Himself on earth through the Church. The Church also *represents* Him on earth during this time of His earthly rejection and absence. Satan has gotten rid of Christ personally from the earth, but He is here *as represented in His people*. To touch the Church or any who belong to it, is to touch Him. Saul had been persecuting the *believers* and yet the Lord's words to him were, "Saul, Saul, why are you persecuting *Me*" (Acts 9:4).

The Church is also God's house, the only house He has on earth at the present time (1 Tim.3:15). God will not be turned out of His own world! Therefore, He dwells today in a house no worldly leader can burn to the ground or destroy.

God's ultimate purpose is to have a bride for Christ (Eph.5:25-27), a people who, although presently sharing His rejection as heavenly strangers, will eternally share His heavenly glory.

We have still other blessings that Israel never had. One of the greatest is the knowledge of God *as Father,* as fully revealed in Christ. "No one has seen God at any time. The only begotten Son who is in the bosom of the Father, *He has declared Him"* (Jn.1:18). Then we have the *fact,* not the *promise,* of accomplished redemption. The I.O.U. has been exchanged for the pure gold of the finished work of Christ. Further, the Holy Spirit now *indwells* believers (Jn.14:16; Acts 2:1-4). Although the Holy Spirit has always exerted His influence on earth, His abiding presence here is a new thing. Also new is our relationship with God. We are no more servants *but sons* (Gal.4:4-7).

Much more could be said, but these four facts should show us something of the wealth of blessing that belongs to us as Christians. *Let us thank God that we live on this side of the cross of Christ!*

∽

Chapter 11

WORSHIP AND SERVICE

Christianity in its practical outworkings is a well-balanced combination of the passive and active sides of our divine life. Every Christian is a *receiver* throughout his life. He must daily sit at Jesus' feet and hear His Word (Lk.10:39) and cultivate that quiet spirit which insures a receptive state. Otherwise, he will have nothing to give out. Then, having received, he finds himself forced by love to give. If we are rejoicing in the knowledge of sins forgiven, our joy will not be complete until we have told someone else. If some fresh scriptural truth has been seen, we will not really know it until we have acted on it. We really possess a truth only when we act on it.

A Christian is like a reservoir: he must have an inlet and an outlet. If he becomes so involved in the *activities* of Christianity that he is always attempting to give out without stopping to take in, spiritual emptiness and poverty will result. If he degenerates into a dreamy mystic who rejects all forms of Christian activity due to a claimed zeal for more divine truth, spiritual excess and disorder will result, and his loss will be great. "From him who does not have, even what he has will be taken away" (Mt.25:29) was said of the servant who *received* a talent, but did not give it out so it could earn interest.

All true Christian activity flows only from the *love of God* as known in the soul. These activities are both those which have God alone as their object and end (worship), and those which have man as their immediate object (service), to God's glory. *Worship,* however, must be first. Since it is a purely spiritual activity *Godward* that gives no tangible benefit to anyone else, it is often greatly neglected and little understood.

If Christians assemble together and draw consciously into the presence of God to pour out their hearts in thanksgiving and worship, many will be ready to rebuke them for their waste of time: "Why was this fragrant oil wasted" (Mk.14:4)? The worshipers will be told to go out and do something that will be of practical benefit to someone else.

Other so-called ministers so completely "set their mind on earthly things" (Phil.3:19) that they have no thoughts for "those things which are above" (Col.3:1), which things the believer is told to seek. Their aim is limited to the material gain of man—a terrible spiritual degradation.

A magazine article described the views of such people as to how a "church" should be run as follows. "By training people in music, developing orators and athletes, starting Bible-classes with heaps of fun and making the church a social center, the writer has created a new community spirit. As a result, land values are going up." Such activities are neither worship nor service. There is *nothing* in them for God, and *nothing* for the *spiritual* benefit of man. Such so-called ministers and churches must have no idea of what *worship* really means.

What is worship? In the Old Testament, the word was often used in a ceremonial sense: "to bow oneself down" was its literal meaning. In the New Testament, the word gets its inward and spiritual meaning with which we are concerned. It means *the up-flow of adoring, responsive love from the believer to God who is now known as "Father."*

In John 4:21-24, the Lord carefully distinguishes between "true worshipers" and worshipers according to the ancient rites. After speaking of the Father as the Object of worship, He adds "God is Spirit, and those who worship Him must worship in spirit and truth" (v.24). The Father is only to be worshiped according to what He has revealed Himself to be. The worship must be *in spirit* because God is Spirit. Thus, true worship is not a matter of religious emotions aroused by impressive ritual and/or music— [things on the level of the soul, Ed.]. The *spirit* is the highest part of man *and unless we worship in spirit, we do not worship at all.*

Our worship must also be "in truth." *Truth* is the realities of God Himself—that which He has revealed Himself to be. The Lord alone could say, "I am ... the truth" (Jn.14:6). He alone is the perfect revelation of God, and it is as *Father* that the Lord has revealed God to us. Therefore, the Lord said, "He who has seen Me has seen the Father" (Jn.14:9). So the *Father is* to be worshiped *in truth,* in the light of that revelation which has come to us in Christ. However, that which does not give Christ His right place is not true worship. Worshiping the Father and rejoicing in Christ Jesus go hand in hand (Phil.3:3).

This is extremely important! It we grasp the fact that true worship *is in spirit, we* will be delivered from the ritualistic idea which thinks God can be worshiped by man's ways—that the more impressive the ceremony, the more grand the surroundings, the more acceptable is the worship. Also, when we realize true worship must be *in truth,* we will be delivered from attempting to worship God by science or the study of God's handiwork in nature. We will seek the essential knowledge of God as revealed in Christ.

After worship comes *service,* the outcome of the gracious activity of divine love in the hearts of believers which leads them to an endless variety of labors for the glory of God and the good of others. Let us make no mistake here! The very basis of true service is, although undertaken so others will be helped, *done for the pleasure of and under the direction of the Lord Jesus Christ.*

Our only motive in service should be to please the Lord who is our great Example in this. Speaking of the Father, He said, "I always do those things that please Him" (Jn.8:29). It is not enough to do *right things. Right things done with a wrong motive are wrong in God's sight.* Neither is it enough to act even with a right motive if we are simply acting on our own thoughts. A worker may be a good workman, but a poor servant. If he is opinionated and independent, he will be constantly running against his boss's wishes and will be in constant trouble. He won't be very useful.

Again, the Lord is our example. In John 4:34, He said, "My food is to do the will of Him who sent Me and to *finish* His work." Service, then, is not simply work, even good work, not even Christian activity of the most scriptural kind, but rather it is such activity *under the direction of the Lord!*

John 12:1-9 provides a good illustration of this. Martha served: she worked on that supper and many benefited by it, but the important point is that she did it *for the Lord.* "They made Him a supper." That was true service done from a heart full of love for the One who had raised her dead brother. Then Lazarus "sat at the table *with Him,*" a type of that communion with the Master which alone gives character to either service or worship. Mary took costly ointment and anointed Jesus' feet (v.3). She poured all of it on Him. It was the outflow of a heart concentrated on Christ. The odor of the ointment filled the house. True worship is fragrant everywhere.

The Father is seeking worshipers (Jn.4:23). The Lord needs servants (2 Tim.2:1-7). May we respond to both desires!

We should have no *form* for worship. The Jews of the previous dispensation did have a certain outward, national, ceremonial form of worship that was acceptable to God if carried out with a right heart. But their hearts were not right, so the Lord had to say that "in vain they worship Me" (Mt.15:9). Our worship today is not national and not a matter of saying certain words or performing certain ceremonies and observances. It is the conscious, personal expression of love and adoration of our *individual* redeemed hearts to God!

Sometimes people speak about worshiping God whenever they go to a *service.* A preacher arose one Lord's Day morning and said, "Let us begin the worship of God by singing the hymn 'Come ye sinners, poor and needy.'" To him, *worship* evidently meant any kind of religious meeting. It does not! It may be a true service to the Lord for someone to conduct a meeting to build up believers or for the salvation of sinners, but it is no "service" for the listeners or any kind of worship for either the preacher or his hearers! Worship is neither hearing nor preaching sermons, nor is it praying or singing gospel hymns. Worship is that up-flow of adoration which arises from a redeemed soul to God, *and nothing else!*

Now, all Christians are both priests and servants. 1 Peter 2:5,9 tells us we "are being built up ... a *holy priesthood* to offer up spiritual sacrifices acceptable to God through Jesus Christ" [and also] "a *royal priesthood* ... that you may *proclaim* the praises of Him who called you out of darkness into His marvelous light." These words were written to all Christians, not to some "clergy." We *all* are both a holy and a royal priesthood. As a holy priesthood, we offer up spiritual sacrifices to God, i.e., worship! As a royal priesthood, we proclaim or show forth the praises of God, i.e., service!

It is true we all don't have a *major* gift according to 1 Corinthians 12:28, nor are we all an evangelist, pastor or teacher according to Ephesians 4:11, but we can all serve according to Romans 12:3-8 [or be a *help* as in 1 Corinthians 12:28, Ed.]. If we cannot prophesy or teach, we can show hospitality and mercy. We can bless our persecutors and weep in sympathy with a weeping saint. We can help whenever needed, and in all these things, be truly serving the Lord.

However, there are some *qualifications* for us to truly worship and serve God. As to worship, Hebrews 10:19-22 speaks of *"boldness* to enter the holiest by the blood of Jesus" and we are exhorted to *draw near to God* with "a true heart in full assurance of faith." These are important qualifications. Faith must be in active exercise so there is *full assurance* based upon the work of Christ—*not a doubt or fear left.* Then, a true heart indicates that sincerity and transparency of soul which is the result of a tender conscience and self-judgment. [Then we can have boldness—no fear—to enter in, Ed.].

As to service, read Acts 20:17-35. Here, Paul, one of the greatest servants of Christ, reviews his career. Our service may be insignificant compared to Paul's, yet the things that characterized him should characterize us. Here are some of them: "all humility," "many tears" (expressive of much exercise), "none of these things moved me" (stability), "I have coveted no one's silver or gold or apparel" (the strictest possible righteousness before the world) and "I have *shown* you in every way" (practicing what he preached). These are important qualifications indeed!

Both young and recently saved believers often wonder how they can serve the Lord. I would encourage them to serve the Lord by simply doing the thing which (in God's ordering of their lives) is needed *next.* "Do the *next* thing" is a very good guide for all of us, even though it may be the very thing we *don't* want to do!

Years ago, a poorly educated servant-girl in Virginia earned only four dollars a month. Of this, one dollar went to her chapel and one dollar to foreign missions. She was the largest local contributor in both these directions. The other two dollars went to her poor father. She clothed herself by taking in sewing at night. An earnest minister visited the home and she gave up her room for him. He opened her Bible, which was on the table, and found it marked on every page. But what most struck him was her note next to "Go into all the world" (Mk.16:15). Her note said "Oh, if I only could!"

Next day, he spoke to her about it, whereupon she began to weep. Finally the story came out. She was saved at the age of 14 and on reaching home, she found a paper, *China's Call for the Gospel*, lying around. Nobody knew where it came from. That paper had colored all her thoughts. For ten years, she had prayed that the Lord would send her to China, but He hadn't.

Lately, she said, a change had come over her. Just two weeks before, she had concluded she had made a mistake and the Lord's plan for her was to simply be a missionary in the kitchen. At once, her prayer became, "Make me willing to be a missionary for Thee in the kitchen," and the Lord had answered that prayer.

For ten years, she had longed for the big thing, even though she had not neglected the smaller things, as her contributions showed. But only lately had she been willing to accept the *very little thing* of simply shining for the Lord in the narrow place of a kitchen-maid. But then the Lord sent her to a life of blessed service in China, for the minister became convinced God had specially sent him there to help her go to China, *and she went.*

May such service be greatly multiplied on every hand! "He who is faithful in what is least is faithful also in much" (Lk.16:10).

∼

Chapter 12

THE RAPTURE AND THE APPEARING

The Lord Jesus Christ is coming back again. Yet many Christians don't really believe it. They see it as a dreamy, mystical idea and think those who enthusiastically proclaim it must be mistaking figures of speech for sober facts.

Since we believe the Lord was here once, then why not again? Look at what happened when He first came about 2000 years ago. He was rejected and murdered. His public mission of 3.5 years ended in death (even though that death wrought redemption for His people). Then He rose from the dead. Do you think *that* story will just end there; that the ejection of the Creator from His world by His creatures will be the last word? By no means! Although people despised Him in His humiliation, He will return in glory, power and authority.

This is not speculation. The doctrine (teaching) of the Second Coming is one of the most common themes of Scripture in both the Old and New Testaments. One of the most definite verses is Acts 1:11, "Men of Galilee, why do you stand gazing up into heaven? The same Jesus who was taken up from you into heaven, will so come in like manner as you saw Him go into heaven." This message sounds like a legal document. Lawyers often write a simple thing in a lengthy way, so nothing can be misinterpreted. Likewise, the angel here uses a fullness of expression to foil any attempt to evade or mystify this great fact.

Thus the Lord Jesus will come again just as He went. How did He go? Personally: He will return personally. As a living Man: He will return as an actual living Man. Visibly: He will return visibly. From the earth: He will return to the earth. From the Mount of Olives: He will return to the Mount of Olives (Zech.14:4; Rev.1:7).

However, as a careful reader reads all the verses on the Lord's second coming, he finds apparent discrepancies in these verses. The key that unlocks this mystery is there are *two parts* or stages to the Lord's second coming. These two parts are often called *The Rapture* (the "catching up") and *The Appearing.*

Carefully read 1 Thessalonians 4:13 to 5:3. Notice the Thessalonian believers were troubled because some of their number had died. They were afraid these dead believers would thus miss the glory of the *appearing* and reign of Christ. But Paul told them not to worry because as surely as Jesus had died and risen again, God would bring *with* Jesus all such when He comes to reign (v.14). Then Paul explains how this is to happen, how the formerly dead-in-Christ will be found with Christ in bodies of glory, so as to be able to share in His glorious appearing and reign.

This explanation is prefaced by "This we say to you by the Word of the Lord," which indicates that what followed had not been previously known, but was *a new and direct revelation from God.*

Now, let's look at the explanation directly from Scripture: "The Lord Himself will descend from heaven with a shout ... and the dead in Christ will rise first. Then we who are alive and remain shall be caught up together with them" (the just resurrected dead believers) "in the clouds to meet the Lord in *the air,* and thus we shall always be with the Lord" (1 Th.4:13-18). Then 1 Corinthians 15:51-54 gives us two more facts—the dead will be raised incorruptible and we who are living at that time will be changed.

Thus, the Lord Himself will descend from heaven into the *atmosphere* (not to the earth) with a great shout. His shout will awaken the dead saints (those asleep in Jesus) and raise them in *bodies of glory* (Phil.3:20-21, JND). We who are living at that moment will also undergo a similar change into a glorified condition. Then both the formerly dead believers and we living believers will be caught up together to be forever with the Lord. Oh, what a blessed moment, the completion of our long-cherished hope!

All this happens in a split second, a "twinkling of an eye" (1 Cor.15:52). The unsaved in the world are untouched except for the mystery of the sudden disappearance of millions of saints. But the hour of God's judgment on the unsaved world soon comes. Hence, the next verses after the description of the Rapture (i.e., 1 Th.5:1-3) distinguish between the just-described Rapture and "the day of the Lord." That day comes, not as a Bridegroom for His bride, but as a "thief *in the night.*"

When the Lord Jesus (in His humiliation, Phil.2:5-8) was led as a lamb to the slaughter, He said to His enemies, "This is *your* hour and the power of darkness" (Lk.22:53).

But the tables are to be completely turned. He will come again to the earth, not in humiliation, but in glory; not as a lamb to the slaughter, but as the Lion of the tribe of Judah; not alone, but with "ten thousands of His saints"; not submitting to the will of His enemies, but to make His enemies His footstool. Then it will be the Lord's great and dreadful day.

"The day of the Lord" (1 Th.5:2) is not a 24-hour day, but an interval of time like the "day of salvation" in which we presently live. It will be characterized by the absolute supremacy and authority of the Lord.

The Old Testament prophets often spoke of this *appearing* because it was the consummation of God's ways with Israel and the earth. Hence, the Lord's appearing begins a short work of judgment to clear the earth of open evil before the shining forth of glory in the millennial (1000 year) reign of Christ, which is closely connected with Israel and Jerusalem as seen in Joel 2:1-2 and Amos 5:18.

However, between the Rapture and the Appearing, certain terrible things must take place on the earth as seen in Matthew 24; Mark 13 and Luke 21. Second Thessalonians 2:3-12 shows that before the day of the Lord comes, there must be "a falling away" (apostasy) and, connected with that apostasy, the revelation of the *man of sin*, commonly called the *Antichrist*. In him, sin will find its highest expression. Then when man's iniquity is at its maximum, God smites in judgment.

The oldest prophecy by any man (Enoch) will then be fulfilled, "Behold the Lord comes with ten thousands of His saints to execute judgment on all" (Jude 14-15).

Because of the Rapture some seven years previously, the saints of our (and previous) dispensations are with the Lord in heaven during this time and therefore will also be with Him when the heavens open to reveal Him in the "flaming fire" of judgment. He will then be "glorified in His saints" and "admired among all those who believe ... in that day" (2 Th.1:7-10). See also Colossians 3:4. Meanwhile, our business is to "serve the living and true God and to wait for His Son from heaven" (1 Th.1:9-10).

Yet Christians will still argue that the Rapture is just a beautiful and poetic way of speaking of a believer's death and that the Appearing is simply what is commonly called "the end of the world." However, a Christian's death is described as departing this world to be with Christ (Phil. 1:23). At death, we go to Him, but He is going to *come* for us. Further, when a saint dies and goes to be with Christ, his body is laid in a grave.

When Christ comes *for* His saints, He takes their bodies *out* of the graves and changes them into never-dying *bodies of glory* (Phil.3:21, JND). Thus, the coming of the Lord *for* His saints (the Rapture) is not death, but the deliverance of God's people from the last trace of death. It is the "redemption of our body" (Rom.8:23).

Neither is the appearing of Christ *with* His saints the "end of the world"—the ending of the heavens and the earth as we know them. Revelation 19 speaks of the Lord's appearing in glory. Chapter 20 shows the result: Satan is bound and 1000 years of great blessing follow for this weary old earth. After *that* comes the end, and then God forms a new heaven and a new earth (Rev.21).

Sometimes the question is asked whether we shouldn't call the Rapture the Lord's *second* coming and the appearing His *third* coming. But it is not spoken of in that way in Scripture. Often His coming is spoken of in a general way without referring definitely to either of its two stages. Thus the Rapture and the Appearing are simply two parts of Christ's one "coming again." At the coming of Christ, we will first be caught up into the air to meet Him, and after a short time of necessary preparation both in heaven and on earth, we will return with Him to share in His glorious kingdom.

We can currently see many signs that indicate the Lord's *appearing* is near at hand, as seen in such scriptures as Matthew 24; 2 Thessalonians 2 and 2 Timothy 3. The rising tide of apostasy in Christendom (the giving up of God's truth), the increasing prevalence of false prophets deceiving many, the re-forming of Israel in 1948 as a sovereign nation, and the Jewish control of Jerusalem (the fig tree putting forth leaves in Matthew 24:32), the ecumenical movement, and the European Union with its common currency, the Euro, in Western Europe, are some of the signs to show us that we are drawing near to the end of this age.

There are, however, *no signs to precede the Rapture.* It is an event outside of the calculation of times and seasons which belong to the earth. There is *nothing* awaiting fulfillment before Christ comes *for* His saints. He may come at any moment! [Since the Rapture is more than seven years before the Appearing and we can *already* see signs that point to the nearness of the Appearing, *how very near the Rapture must be*, Ed.].

Many believers think the world must be converted to God before the Lord can even come for His saints. *Nowhere does the Bible even imply that the whole world will be converted by the preaching of the gospel!* The gospel is preached at God's command for the gathering out from the nations a people for His Name (Acts 15:14).

The whole world will not be converted by this preaching, but rather will be *purified by judgment, which* will remove the workers of evil and bring the world into subjection to God. "When Your *judgments*" (not Your gospel) "are in the earth, the inhabitants of the world will learn righteousness" (Isa.26:9).

A question often asked is whether all Christians will be caught up at the Rapture. The answer is yes. To illustrate, hold a strong magnet above some iron filings mixed with sand. The iron will be drawn up, the sand left behind. But Christians are more than just individual iron filings. By the Holy Spirit, they are in living connection with each other. They are one flock, one family, one body. When the Lord Jesus comes, He will take His Church as one living entity, His body and His bride. Mutilated fragments will not be left behind.

The idea that some will be left behind comes from two sources. First, some false teachers teach that only living, faithful and *watching* Christians will be taken. Their "faithfulness" is shown by their reception of the teachings of the false teacher in question! Comment on this is needless. Secondly, true Christians have read Hebrews 9:28, "To *those who eagerly wait for Him,* He will appear a second time, apart from sin, for salvation" and come away with the idea that only *watching* believers are caught up at the Rapture.

But can you find a true Christian who isn't looking for Christ? Some may know nothing about the Rapture, yet they look for Christ. He is the hope of their hearts even though they don't know how that hope will be fulfilled. The fact is, the expression "those who eagerly wait for Him" is equal to "those who love God" (Rom.8:28): they both are just the Bible-way of describing believers. If someone doesn't love God or look for Christ, he cannot be called a Christian. [The above verse speaks of the Rapture even though the word *appear* is used. Here Christ appears only to believers; when He appears to reign, *every* eye shall see Him (Rev.1:7), Ed.].

Many believers feel the second coming is a rather speculative truth and shouldn't be emphasized. That is not true! It is no more speculative than the truth divinely given to Noah concerning the approaching flood, or than the prophecies given to Israel concerning the first coming of their Messiah. Difficulties may be raised as to details where Scripture is silent, but the broad outline of the truth stands clear and plain in Scripture and the event is sure.

In fact, the truth of the Rapture *should* be emphasized because the event itself is near. Foolish and unscriptural attempts have been made to fix dates, and earnest Christians have foolishly used extravagant language, giving the impression that the Rapture couldn't be more than a year or two away. Then years passed. Consequently, many who listened to those extravagant claims have become skeptical of the whole thing. But the truth of His imminent (very soon) return remains. Everything in both the Church and the world point to the ending of this age. Therefore, we should be lifting up our heads and expecting Him [while at the same time not neglecting all the work in which He has directed us, Ed.].

The other day I saw a motto in a friend's house which said "Perhaps Today." I knew what it meant. That is the right attitude. Since His coming is certainly near, we should rise up each morning with the thought that *perhaps He will come today.* May we so purify ourselves in holiness before Him, that our unquestioning response may gladly be, "Even so, come, Lord Jesus."

F.B. Hole (Edited)

NOTES

For an updated listing of our select Christian literature please visit:

<u>www.bbusa.org</u>

You may also contact us at:

Believers Bookshelf, Inc.
P. O. Box 261
Sunbury, Pennsylvania 17801
USA

CPSIA information can be obtained at www.ICGtesting.com
Printed in the USA
BVOW07s1248111214

378528BV00001B/3/P